ગયુ કે આ દેશની નૈસર્ગિક વિશિષ્ટતા તેના હિંદુ હોવાપણાંમાં રહેલી છે, જે હિંદુઇઝીમની આધ્યામિકતા છે. એક સામાન્ય હિંદુ, જેને તમે કોઇ પણ સ્થળે હજારો ગામડાંમાં મળો છો. તે એક સાદો માનવી છે અને તેનામાં આંતરિલ આધ્યાત્મકતા છે અને તે તમને તમે જેવા છો તેવા સ્વીકારી લેશે, ભલે તમે ખ્રિસ્તી કે મુસ્લિમ, જૈન કે આરબ કે ફ્રેંચ કે ચાઇનીઝ હોવ. આ હિંદુઇઝીમ જ છે જેને લીધે ભારતીય ખ્રિસ્તીઓ, ફ્રેંચ ખ્રિસ્તીઓ કે ભારતીય મુસ્લિમો કે સાઉદી મુસ્લિમોથી અલગ પડે છે, હું એ પણ શીખ્યો છું કે હિંદુઓ માને છે કે દૈવીશક્તિ એ જ સ્વરૂપે પ્રગટ થાય છે, ભલે તે સમય કે તેનાં નામો જુદાં જુદાં હોય. (તેમાં અવતારની વિભાવનાઓ પણ આવી જાય છે, જે ૨૧મી સદીના ધર્મનો સંપૂર્ણ ઉત્તર છે), ઉપરાંત તેઓએ વિશ્વની અનેક જુલમોની ભોગ બનેલ જાતિઓને આશ્રય આપ્યો છે - જેમાં સિરિયાના ખ્રિસ્તીઓ, આદિવાસીઓ - એમાંના કેટલાક તો ખ્રિસ્તીમાં પરિવર્તન પામેલા અને બીજાઓ હોય છે. તેમ છતાં બાબરી મસ્જિદને તોડી નાખવામાં આવી ત્યારે કોઇ મુસ્લિમની હત્યા કરવામાં આવી ન હતી; જયારે તેની સરખામણીમાં ૧૯૯૩ના બૉમ્બિંગ સમયે હજારો વ્યક્તિઓ, જેમાં મોટાભાગની હિંદુ હતી તેઓની હત્યા કરવામાં આવી હતી.

મૂળ લેખકઃ ફ્રાંકોઇસ ગૌટિયર
અનુવાદ : ડૉ. પ્રદીપ પંડ્યા

તેમ છતાં બાબરી મસ્જિદને તોડવાની ક્રિયાને આ બન્ને બનાવોમાં સૌથી વધારે ભયંકર પ્રેસ દ્વારા કહેવામાં આવે છે. અમને એ પણ યાદ છે કે ૧૯૯૩માં મહારાષ્ટ્રમાં જ્યારે કોઇ બૉમ્બ મુસ્લિમ વિસ્તારમાં ફાટવાનો હતો ત્યારે તે સમયના મુખ્ય પ્રધાન શરદ પવાર જુઠ્ઠું બોલ્યા હતા.

હું દરેક સમયે રાજકીય રીતે સાચો નથી હોતો પણ મેં હંમેશાં એ જ લખ્યું છે જે મને શોધ દરમિયાન મળ્યું છે. તો પછી મને આ કહેવાતા હિંદુ આંતકવાદ માટે બૉમ્બધડાકાઓમાં હજારો નિર્દોષ હિંદુઓ માર્યા ગયા છે. આ દેશમાં જ્યાં હિંદુઓની બહુમતી છે ત્યાં તેઓની મશ્કરી થાય છે, તેઓને ધીક્કારવામાં આવે છે અને તેઓ જયારે અમરનાથની યાત્રાએ જાય ત્યારે તેઓને મૂળભૂત સગવડો પણ આપવામાં આવતી નથી., જ્યારે હજ પર જનારાઓને વધુમાં વધુ સહાયતા આપવામાં આવે છે. તેઓ જુએ છે કે તેઓના ભાઇ-બહેનોને નાણાંની અને બીજી લાલચ આપીને ખ્રિસ્તી બનાવવામાં આવે છે, તેઓ જુએ છે કે એક નિર્દોષ ૮૪ વર્ષનાં સાધુ-સાધ્વીની ક્રૂરતાપૂર્વક હત્યા થાય છે. તેઓના ઇશ્વરની મશ્કરી થાય છે. તેથી એમ કહેવું પડે કે હવે બસ થયું. બસ થયું.

કોઇ એક બિન્દુએ, સદીઓ સુધી ઘેટાંની જેમ કતલ થતા હિંદુઓ, જેને મહાત્માએ એક વખત નરમાસથી કાયર કહ્યા હતા-બેકાબૂ બની જાય છે આ બહુ લાગી આવે છે. આમ કોઇની નેતાગીરીથી.

તેથી બીજેપીએ એકબીજા સાથે લડવાને બદલે કે બીજો પ્રમુખ કોણ બનશે કે ૨૦૧૪માં વડા પ્રધાનનો ઉમેદવાર કોણ હશે તેની ચર્ચા કરવાને બદલે તેઓનાં ઘરને વ્યવસ્થિત કરવાની જરૂર છે, કારણકે એક વાત તો ચોખ્ખી સમજાય તેવી છે કે આવી યોજના એક મૂર્ખામીભરી, બિનજરૂરી અને ફક્ત નરેન્દ્ર મોદીને બદનામ કરવા માટેની જ છે, જે તેઓના એક નંબરના દુઃશ્મન છે.

તેણે અસત્યનો સામનો સત્યથી કરવો જોઇએ, તે પાસે સો કરોડ હિંદુઓ છે, પૃથ્વી પર દરેક છ માંથી તેઓ સૌથી વધુ સફળ, કાય પાલન કરનાર અને એકમ ધરાવતી કોમ વિશ્વમાં છે. તેઓને આતંકવાદી કહી શકો ? બીજેપીએ ૧૯૪૭ પછી શ કરવી જોઇએ કે હિંદુઓ મુસ્લિમોની કેટલી હત્યા અને મુસ્લિમોએ હિંદુઓની. જ તેઓને સાચી વાત કહેશે

ફ્રાંકોઇસ ગૌટિયર.

Rewriting Indian History

This book does not pretend to be a historical treatise, either on India, or on other civilisations. It only uses events and people in an attempt to go beyond the superficial views that have usually been held on India by many historians.

Rewriting Indian History

François Gautier

> French Journalist and Philosopher Francois Gautier put it best who said "Oh Member of the Indian Intelligentsia! You think that reading the latest New York Times bestseller, speaking polished English, and putting down your own countrymen, especially anybody who has a Hindu connection, makes you an intellectual? But in the process you have not only lost your roots, you have turned your back on a culture and civilisation that is thousands of years old and has given so much to the world. Cry O my beloved India, look what thy children have done to thee!"

(13 July 2012 Fri)

India Research Press
New Delhi

Published by

India Research Press
B-4/22, Safdarjung Enclave, New Delhi – 110 029.
Ph.: 4694610; Fax : 4618637
e-mail : bahrisons@vsnl.com
www.indiaresearchpress.com
2003

2003 © India Research Press

ISBN : 81-87943-27-0

All rights reserved by publisher. No part of this publication unless used for Research & Documentation, may be reproduced, stored in or introduced into a retrieval system or transmitted in any form, or by any means, electronic, mechanical, photocopying, recording or otherwise, without the prior written permission of the publisher of this book..

Cataloging in Publication Data
François Gautier
Rewriting Indian History
by François Gautier

Includes bibliographical references and index.
1. History. 2. Indian History. 3. South Asia
4. Title 5. Author

Printed in India by Focus Impressions, New Delhi – 110 003.

India Research Press
B-4/22, Safdarjung Enclave, New Delhi – 110 029
Ph.: 4694610 Fax : 4618637
e-mail : bahrisons@vsnl.com
www.indiaresearchpress.com

Dedicated to my mother, Andree Gautier.

INTRODUCTION

India's history was mostly written on the basis of archaeological and linguistic discoveries made by the British in colonial times, or by historians employed by the British, such as Max Mueller. But the British, who were the Masters in India, had a vested interest to show that Indian civilisation was not as ancient and as great as it was earlier thought. For, up to the 18th century, philosophers and thinkers in Europe, such as Voltaire, Hegel and even as late as Nietzsche, kept referring to Indian philosophy and science as the mother of all philosophies and sciences.

This is why the British established a two-pronged strategy: first to postdate most of Indian history, such as the creation of the Vedas, for instance, which was brought down to 1200 BC, from a much more ancient date; and two, to show that whatever was good in India –Sanskrit, philosophy, architecture, literature - came from the West, via the Aryan invasion. For this purpose, consciously, or unconsciously, a number of "discoveries" were made, such as the finding of skeletons by Mortimer Wheeler in Mohenja-Daro, which prompted him to hastily conclude that Aryans had "massacred" Dravidians, while invading India, so as to establish these myths of Indian history which have endured till today and have been, unfortunately, blindly adopted by Indian historians and taught to Indian children.

Luckily today, a lot of new archaeological and linguistic discoveries have totally shattered many of the myths on which rests India's History. The mapping of the Saraswati river bed by satellite photography, for instance, shows that there was an Indian civilisation much prior to the Indus Valley culture – hence most of India's history pointers will have soon to be predated; the possible decipherment of the Harappan script, if proved right, would establish that there never was an Aryan civilisation, but that on the contrary, in ancient times, a tremendous amount of movement went from India, not only eastwards, where Hinduism and Buddhism established a strong presence, right up to China, but also westwards via Persia, where it formulated the Zoroastrian religion, right up to Europe, where the Gypsies of today are one of those lost Indian tribes; and that the results of this migration can be seen in the making of Egyptian pyramids, the formulating of Greek philosophy and mathematics, or even the legends of the Celts.

Thus, it is becoming increasingly clear that India's history has to be rewritten. The Aryan invasion, for example, has divided India along ethnic lines and pitted the so-called Dravidians against the supposed Aryans, without any real basis. Even Western history would have then to be rewritten, because, for instance, the myth of Hitler's pure Germanic race stands totally shattered: the true Aryans are not blue-eyed, blond specimens, but ordinary Indians, whether the Tamil, dark-skinned because of the hot geographic conditions of the South, or the Kashmiri, fairer looking owing to the genetic modifications of his ancestors having lived for thousands of year in a colder climate.

This attempt at rewriting history is of course meeting with a lot of resistance on the part of those who have a vested interest in keeping Indian history under wraps, as well as those who for decades have taught and written books and articles which blindly copied the British version. But nevertheless, unless it is done truthfully, however painful it could be for certain sections of India's vast ethnic and religious mosaic, India will never be able to face squarely its own history and evolve a justified pride in its great and ancient civilisation.

Contents

Introduction	vii
1. The Spirit of Colombus Survives	1
2. The First Disinformation on India: The Aryan Invasion	5
3. The Second Disinformation : The Vedas	9
4. The Third Disinformation: The Caste System	15
5. The Greatness of Ancient India	19
6. Islam in India	37
7. The Ugly European Colonies	41
8. Swaraj	49
9. 15th August 1947	63
10. XXth Century India : A Self Denial	73
11. The Bharatiya Janata Party Years	87
12. The Threats at the Hands of Indian Themselves	97
13. The Threats from India's Neighbours	117
14. The Hindus are also to Blame	131
15. The Real India	143
16. India the Spiritual Leader of the World	151
17. Bibliography	159

Chapter 1

The Spirit of Colombus Survives

A civilisation is like the human soul: it has a childhood, where it struggles to learn; an adolescence where it discovers - sometimes painfully - the hard facts of life; an adulthood, where it enjoys the fruits of maturity; and an old age, which slowly leads to death and oblivion.

In this manner, since the dawn of human history, civilisations have risen, reached their zenith where they remain for some time, achieving their enduring excellence and then slowly began their descent towards extinction. Usually, old age for these civilisations meant that they fell prey to barbarians, because they had lost the vitality and the inner obedience to their particular genius, which they had possessed at the time of their peak and which had protected them. This has been a natural process and barbarians have played an important role in the evolution of humanity, for they made sure, in the most ruthless manner, that civilisations did not stagnate; because, like a human being, a civilisation must die many times before it realises the fullness of its soul and attains divine perfection.

There have been many such great civilisations which rose and fell throughout the ages: Mesopotamia, Egypt, India, Africa, China, Greece, or Rome. Human nature being what it is, most of these civilisations established their might by military conquest and thus imposed their order and their views upon others, a process which some have called civilisation, others colonisation.

The advent of Jesus Christ heralded the rise of the European-Western civilisation, whose forerunners were the Greek and Roman cultures. For a long time, Europe was only a lot of disunited barbarian tribes fighting each other. The Crusades signalled the earliest attempt at unity, although the French and the British, for instance, kept warring each other long after them. Some of these nations were great seafarers. Thus Spain and Portugal, for instance, reached out to the far world and colonised huge chunks of territories in the Americas from the 14th century onwards. But it can be safely said that with the industrial revolution, European civilisation started reaching its maturity at the beginning of the 19th century and that a great civilisation, whose genius was consciousness in the material, developed henceforth. Simultaneously, of course, as all other civilisations had done before, Europe started expanding outwards and imposed its own civilisation on other cultures, which had lost their vitality and were open to conquest. England, particularly, because it mastered the seas, went farther, faster and acquired more territories than other European nations, such as France, who often had to settle for the crumbs. And certainly, Great Britain's prize possession, the jewel of its colonies, must have been India, whose mighty borders extended then from Afghanistan to Cape Comorin.

Western civilisation must be intimately associated with Christianity, even though Christianity took different forms over the ages: Protestantism, Lutheranism, Russian Orthodoxy. According to the Hindus, Jesus Christ was an "avatar", a direct emanation from God. Christ was surely a great avatar of love and Christianity certainly had a softening influence on the Western world, where, let's face it, barbarism was the order of the day for many centuries. In the Middle Ages for instance, Christianity was the only island of sanity in a world of rape,

The Spirit of Colombus Survives

black plague, murders and chaos; and as the Brahmins did in India, it was the Christians who preserved the oral and written word for posterity. There have been many great saints in Christianity, men of wisdom, who strove for divine vision in austerity. Such were Saint Francis of Assisi, who reached high spiritual experience, Saint Vincent de Paul, who practised true Christian charity, or Saint Gregory, who attained authentic knowledge. Unfortunately, Christianity got somehow politicised and fossilised under the influence of corrupt Popes and has often become a magma of dogmas, rites, do's and dont's.

Generally, because all Christians believed - like the Muslims - that only their God was the true one, the Christian colonialists sought to impose upon the people they conquered their own brand of religion, and they used the military authority of their armies to do so. It is true that this was done in good faith, that the "soldiers of Christ" thought that the civilisations they stumbled upon were barbarous, pagan and incomprehensible. True also that they sincerely believed that they brought upon these "savages" the virtues of western civilisation: medicine, education and spiritual salvation. But the harm done by Christian missionaries all over the earth will never be properly assessed. In South America, the Spanish soldiers and priests annihilated, in the name of Jesus, an entire civilisation, one of the brightest ever, that of the Incas and the Aztecs. Everywhere the Christians went, they stamped mercilessly on cultures, eradicated centuries old ways of life, to replace them with totally inadequate systems, crude, Victorian, moralistic, which slowly killed the spontaneity of life of the people they conquered. They were thus able to radically alter civilisations, change their patterns of thinking. And three generations later the children of those who had been conquered, had forgotten their roots, adapted Christianity and often looked upon their conquerors as their benefactors.

Yet, every year, the West celebrates the anniversary of

Columbus, discoverer of the "New World" with fanfare and pomp. But the New World was already quite old when it was discovered by the young barbarians, much older in fact than the fledgling Western civilisation. And Columbus, however courageous and adventurous, was a ruthless man, whose sighting of the New World triggered an unparalleled rape in human history.

Yet, not only the West still deifies Columbus, but no one in the Third World has been capable of challenging coherently that undeserved status.

The truth is that today, not only in the Western world, but also in the entire so-called developing world, we are constantly looking at things and events through a prism that has been fashioned by centuries of western thinking. And as long as we do not get rid of that tainted glass we will not understand rightly the world in general and India in particular.

For the stamp of Western civilisation will still take some time to be eradicated. By military conquest or moral assertiveness, the West imposed upon the world its ways of thinking; and it created enduring patterns, subtle disinformations and immutable grooves, which play like a record that goes on turning, long after its owner has attained the age of decline. The barbarians who thought they had become "civilised", are being devoured by other barbarians. But today, economic might has replaced the military killing machine.

Chapter 2

The First Disinformation on India : The Aryan Invasion

The theorem of the Aryan invasion is still taken as the foundation stone of the history of India. According to this theory, which was actually devised in the 18th and 19th century by British linguists and archaeologists, who had a vested interest to prove the supremacy of their culture over the one of the subcontinent, the first inhabitants of India were good-natured, peaceful, dark-skinned shepherds, called the Dravidians. They were supposedly remarkable builders, witness the city of Mohenjo-Daro in Pakistani Sind, but had no culture to speak-off, no written texts, no proper script even. Then, around 1500 B.C., India is said to have been invaded by tribes called the Aryans : white-skinned, nomadic people, who originated somewhere in Ural, or the Caucasus. To the Aryans are attributed Sanskrit, the Vedic or Hindu religion, India's greatest spiritual texts, the Vedas, as well as a host of subsequent writings, the Upanishads, the Mahabharata, the Ramanaya, etc.

This was indeed a masterly stroke on the part of the British : thanks to the Aryan theory, they showed on the one hand that Indian civilisation was not that ancient and that it was posterior to the cultures which influenced the western world - Mesopotamia, Sumeria, or Babylon - and on the other hand, that whatever good things India had developed - Sanskrit, literature, or even its architecture, had been influenced by the West. Thus, Sanskrit, instead of being the mother of all Indo-European languages, became just a branch of their huge family; thus, the religion of Zarathustra is said to have influenced Hinduism - as these Aryan tribes were believed to have transited through numerous countries, Persia being one, before reaching India - and not vice versa. In the same manner, many achievements were later attributed to the Greek invasion of Alexander the Great : scientific discoveries, mathematics, architecture etc. So ultimately, it was cleverly proved that nothing is Indian, nothing really great was created in India, it was always born out of different influences on the subcontinent.

To make this theory even more complicated, the British, who like other invaders before them had a tough time with the Brahmins and the Kshatriyas, implied that the Aryans drove the Dravidians southwards, where they are still today; and that to mark forever their social boundaries, these Aryans had devised the despicable caste system, whereby they, the priests and princes, ruled over the merchants and labourers. And thus English missionaries-and later American preachers were able to convert tribes and low caste Hindus by telling them: " you, the aborigines, the tribals, the Harijans, were there in India before the Aryans; you are the original inhabitants of India, and you should discard Hinduism, the religion of these arrogant Aryans, and embrace Christianity, the true religion".

Thus was born the great Aryan invasion theory, of two civilisations, that of the low caste Dravidians and the high caste Aryans, always pitted against each other - which has endured, as it is still today being used by some Indian politicians - and has been enshrined in all history books - Western, and unfortunately also Indian. Thus were born wrong "nationalistic" movements, such as the Dravidian movement against Hindi and the much-maligned Brahmins, who actually represent today a minority, which is often underprivileged. This Aryan invasion theory has also made India look westwards, instead of taking pride in its past and present achievements. It may also unconsciously be one of the reasons why there is such great fascination for Sonia Gandhi, a white-skinned-Westerner, who may be unconsciously perceived as a true Aryan by the downtrodden Dravidians and a certain fringe of that Indian intelligentsia which is permanently affected by an inferiority complex towards the West. It may even have given a colour fixation to this country, where women will go to extremes to look "fair".

But today, this theory is being challenged more and more by new discoveries, both archaeological and linguistic. There are many such proofs, but two stand out : the discovery of the Saraswati river and the deciphering of the Indus seals. In the Rig Veda, the Ganges, India's sacred river, is only mentioned once, but the mythic Saraswati is praised on more than fifty occasions. Yet for a long time, the Saraswati river was considered a myth, until the American satellite Landstat was able to photograph and map the bed of this magnificent river, which was nearly fourteen kilometres wide, took its source in the Himalayas, flowed through the states of Haryana, Punjab and Rajasthan, before throwing itself in the sea near Bhrigukuccha, today called Broach. American archaeologist Mark Kenoyer was able to prove in 1991 that the majority of archaeological sites of the so-called Harappan (or Dravidian) civilisation were not situated on the ancient bed of the Indus river, as first thought, but on the Saraswati. Another archaeologist, Paul-Henri Francfort, Chief of a franco-american mission (Weiss, Courty, Weterstromm, Guichard, Senior, Meadow, Curnow), which studied the Saraswati region at the beginning of the nineties, found out why the Saraswati had 'disappeared' : "around 2200 B.C.," he writes, "an immense drought reduced the whole region to aridity and famine" (Evidence for Harappan irrigation system in Haryana and Rajasthan -Eastern Anthropologist 1992). Thus around this date, most inhabitants moved away from the Saraswati to settle on the banks of the Indus and Sutlej rivers. During the

January 2000 earthquake in Gujurat, parts of the Saraswati river, which runs underground, came-up for some time, before sinking back into the earth, another proof of the existence of the "mythical" Saraswati.

According to official history, the Vedas were composed around 1500 BC, some even say 1200 BC. Yet, as we have seen, the Rig Veda describes India as it was before the great drought which dried up the Saraswati; which means in effect that the so-called Indus or Harappan civilisation was a continuation of the Vedic epoch, which ended approximately when the Saraswati dried up. Recently, the famous Indus seals, discovered on the site of Mohenjo Daro and Harappa, may have been deciphered by Dr Rajaram, a mathematician who worked at one time for the NASA and Dr Jha, a distinguished linguist. In the biased light of the Aryan invasion theory, these seals were presumed to be written in a Harappan (read Dravidian) script, although they had never been convincingly decoded. But Rajaram and Jha, using an ancient Vedic glossary, the Nighantu, found out that the script is of Sanskrit lineage, is read from left to right and does not use vowels (which as in Arabic, are 'guessed' according to the meaning of the whole sentence). In this way, they have been able to decipher so far 1500 to 2000 seals, or about half the known corpus. As with the discovery of the Saraswati river, the decipherment of the Indus scripts also goes to prove that that the Harappan civilisation, of which the seals are a product, belonged to the latter part of the Vedic Age and had close connections with Vedantic works like the Sutras and the Upanishads.

In this light, it becomes evident that not only was there never an Aryan invasion of India, but, as historian Konraad Elst writes, it could very well be that it was an Indian race which went westwards : " rather than Indo-Iranians on their way from South Russia to Iran and partly to India, these may well be the Hitites, Kassites or Mitanni, on their way from India, via the Aral Lake area, to Anatolia, or Mesopotamia, where they show up in subsequent centuries" (Indigenous Indians).

Chapter 3

The Second Disinformation
The Vedas

The second piece of disinformation concerns the Vedic religion. Ah, the Vedas! So much misconception, so many prejudices, so much distortion has been spewed about this monument of a book, this unparalleled epic. French historian Danielou, for instance, maintains that the original Vedas "were an oral Dravidian tradition, which was reshaped by the Aryans and later put down in Sanskrit". According to Danielou, the Mahabarata is the story of how the low caste Dravidians, the Pandavas, revolted against the high caste Aryans, the Kauravas, who had enslaved them during their conquest and won, helped by the dark-skinned Krishna, a Dravidian of course. Danielou finds lineage between the Vedic religion and the Persian religion (Zarathustra), as well as the Greek Gods; the problem is that he seems to imply that the Vedic religion may have sprung from the Zoroastrian creed! He also puts down all Vedic symbols as purely physical signs: for instance Agni is the fire that should always burn in the house's altar. Finally, he sees in the Rig-Veda "only a remarkable document on the mode of life, society and history of the Aryans".(Histoire de l'Inde, page 62)

But Danielou must be the mildests of all critics. The real disinformation started again with the missionnaries, who saw in the Vedas "the root of the evil", the source of paganism and went systematically about belittling it. The Jesuits, in their dialectical cleverness, brought it down to a set of pagan offerings without great importance. Henceforth, this theory was perpetuated by most Western historians, who not only stripped the Vedas of any spiritual value, but actually post-dated them to approximately 1500 to 1000 years B.C. It is very unfortunate that these theories have been taken-up blindly and without trying to ascertain their truth, by many Indian historians and sociologists such as Romila Tharpar.

And even when more enlightened foreigners like Max Mueller, whose Sanskrit scholarship cannot be denied, took up the Vedas, they only saw "that it is full of childish, silly, even monstrous conceptions, that it is tedious, low, commonplace, that it represents human nature on a low level of selfishness and worldliness and that only here and there are a few rare sentiments that come from the depths of the soul".

If there ever was one who disagreed with the Western view, be it of Danielou, or Max Mueller on the Vedas, it was Sri Aurobindo : "I seek not science, not religion, not theosophy, but Veda, the truth about Brahman, not only about His essentiality, but also about His manifestation, not a lamp on the way to the forest, but a light and a guide to joy and action in the world, the truth which is beyond opinion, the knowledge which all thought strives after -'yasmin vijnate sarvam vijnatam' (which being known, all is known). I believe that Veda be the foundation of the Sanatan Dharma; I believe it to be the concealed divinity within Hinduism, but a veil has to be drawn aside, a curtain has to be lifted. I belive it to be knowable and discoverable. I believe the future of India and the world depends on its discovery and on its application, not to the renunciation of life, but to life in the world and among men". (India's Rebirth, page 90).

Sri Aurobindo contended that Europeans have seen in the Vedas "only the rude chants of an antique and pastoral race sung in honor of the forces of nature and succeeded in imposing them on the Indian intellect". But he insisted that a time must come "when the Indian mind will shake off the darkness that has fallen upon it, cease to think or hold opinions at second and third hand and reassert its right to judge and enquire in perfect freedom into the meaning of its own scriptures". He argued that the Veda remains the foundation of Indian culture: "the Veda was the beginning of our spiritual knowledge, the Veda will remain its end. The recovery of the perfect truth of the Veda is therefore not merely a desideratum for our modern intellectual curiosity, but a practical necessity for the future of the human race. For I firmly believe that the secret concealed in the Veda, when entirely discovered, will be found to formulate perfectly that knowledge and practice of divine life to which the march of humanity, after long wanderings in the satisfaction of the intellect and senses, must inevitably return." (India's rebirth, 94)

What is the secret of the Vedas? First we have to discard the ridiculously early dates given by historians and bring it back to at least 4000 BC. Why did historians show such an eagerness in post-dating the Vedas and making of them just a mumble-jumble of pagan superstition? Because it would have destroyed the West's idea of its own supremacy: primitive barbarism could not possibly have risen to such high conceptions so early, particularly when the Westerners have started our era after the birth of Christ and decreed that the world began on 23rd October 4004 B.C.!

Secondly, the Vedic seers, who had attained the ultimate truth, had clothed their oral findings in symbols and images, so that only the initiated would understand the true meaning of their aphorisms. For the more ordinary souls, "those who were not yet twice born", it meant only an outer worship which was fit for their level of spiritual evolution. The Vedic rituals have lost their profound meaning for us. Therefore, as

Sri Aurobindo elucidates, when we read: "Sarama by the path of the Truth discovers the herds", the mind is stopped and baffled by an unfamiliar language. It has to be translated for us into a plainer and less figured thought: "Intuitions by the way of Truth arrive at the hidden illuminations". (India's rebirth, 109). Lacking the clues, we only see in the Vedas a series of meaningless mouthings about the herds or the Sun. Sri Aurobindo remarks that the Vedic rishis "may not have yoked the lightning to their chariots, nor weighed sun and star, nor materialised all the destructive forces of Nature to aid them in massacre and domination, but they had measured and fathomed all the heavens and earth within us, they had cast their plummet into the inconscient and the subconscient and the supraconscient; they had read the riddle of death and found the secret of immortality; they had sought for and discovered the One and known and worshipped Him in the glories of His light and purity and wisdom and power". (India's rebirth, 116).

Ah, these are the two secrets of the Vedas, then, the reason why they have remained so obscure and lost their original meaning. Firstly, the Vedic rishis had realised that God is One, but He takes many faces in His manifestation; this is the very foundation of Hinduism. And secondly, the Vedic rishis had gone down in their minds and their bodies all the way to the roots of Death, to that eternal question which haunts humanity since the beginning of times: why death? What is the purpose of living if one has always to die? Why the inevitable decay and oblivion? And there, in their own bodies, at the bottom rock of the Inconscient, they had discovered the secret of immortality, which Sri Aurobindo called later the Supramental and which he said was the next step in humanity's evolution… "Not some mysterious elixir of youth, but the point, the spring where All is One and death disappears in the face of the Supreme Knowledge and Ananda." (India's rebirth, 95).

The Second Disinformation : The Vedas

Is this then the work of a few uncivilised sheperds, who had colonised the poor Dravidians? No wonder the West cannot recognise the Vedas for what they are, the whole foundation of their moral domination would then collapse.

All the subsequent scriptures of Hinduism derive from the Vedas, even though some of them lost sight of the original Vedic sense. The Vedas are the foundations of Indian culture; the greatest power of the Vedic teaching, that which made it the source of all later Indian philosophies, religions, systems of yoga, lay in its application to the inner life of man. Man lives in the physical cosmos, subject to death and the falsehood of mortal existence. To rise beyond death, to become one of the immortals, he has to turn from the falsehood to the Truth; he has to turn onto the Light, to battle with and conquer the powers of Darkness. This he does by communion with the Divine Powers and their aid; the way to call down these aids was the secret of the vedic mystics. "The symbols of the outer sacrifice are given for this purpose in the manner of the Mysteries all over the world an inner meaning; they represent a calling of the Gods into the human being, a connecting sacrifice, an intimate interchange, a mutual aid, a communion".(Foundations of Indian Culture. p 145). Sri Aurobindo also emphasises that the work that was done in this period became the firm bedrock of India's spirituality in later ages and from it "gush still the life-giving waters of perennial never failing inspiration".

Chapter 4

The Third Disinformation : The Caste System

The caste system has been the most misunderstood, the most vilified aspect of Hindu society at the hands of Western scholars - and even today by "secular" Indians. And this has greatly contributed to India's self-depreciation, as you hardly find any Indian who is not ashamed of caste, especially if he talks to a Westerner. But ultimately, one must understand the original purpose behind the caste system, as spelt out by India's Great Sage and Avatar of the Modern Age, Sri Aurobindo : "Caste was originally an arrangement for the distribution of functions in society, just as much as class in Europe, but the principle on which this distribution was based was peculiar to India. A Brahmin was a Brahmin not by mere birth, but because he discharged the duty of preserving the spiritual and intellectual elevation of the race, and he had to cultivate the spiritual temperament and acquire the spiritual training which alone would qualify him for the task. The Kshatriya was Kshatriya not merely because he was the son of warriors and princes, but because he discharged the duty of protecting the country and preserving the high courage and manhood of action, and he had to cultivate the princely temperament and acquire the strong and lofty Samurai training which alone fitted him for his duties. So it was for the Vaishya whose function was to amass wealth for the race and the Shudra who discharged the humbler duties of service without which the other castes could not perform their share of labour for the common good". (India's Rebirth, p 26).

It is true that in time the caste system has become perverted, as Sri Aurobindo also noted : "it is the nature of human institutions to degenerate; there is no doubt that the institution of caste degenerated. It ceased to be determined by spiritual qualifications which, once essential, have now come to be subordinate and even immaterial and is determined by the purely material tests of occupation and birth... By this change it has set itself against the fundamental tendency of Hinduism which is to insist on the spiritual and subordinate the material and thus lost most of its meaning. The spirit of caste arrogance, exclusiveness and superiority came to dominate it instead of the spirit of duty, and the change weakened the nation and helped to reduce us to our present condition." (India's Rebirth, p 27).

Today, the abuses being done in the name of caste are often horrifying, specially to a Westerner brought up on more egalitarian values. Some of the backward villages of Tamil Nadu, or Bihar for instance, still segregate Harijans and the lower castes, who do not have the same access to educational facilities as the upper castes, in spite of Nehru's heavy-handed quota system, which has been badly taken advantage off.

Modern-day Indian politicians have exploited, like nobody else, the caste divide for their own selfish purposes. The politicians of ancient India were princes and kings belonging to the Kshatriya caste; their duty was to serve the nation and high ideals were held in front of them by the Brahmins and rishis who advised them. The Buddha's father, for instance, was a king elected by his own people. But today we see corrupt, inefficient men, who have forgotten that they are supposed to serve the nation first, who are only interested in minting the maximum money in the minimum time. Indian politicians have often become a caricature, which is made fun of by the whole country, adding to India's self-negating image. They are frequently uneducated, gross people, elected on the strength of demagogic pledges, such as promising rice for 2 Rupees a kilo, a folly which at one time was draining many state's coffers, or by playing Muslims against Hindus, Harijans against Brahmins, as in the states of Uttar Pradesh and Bihar.

The Third Disinformation : The Caste System

Ministers in India are most of the time ignorant, unqualified, often having no idea about the department they are overseeing - it is the civil servants who control matters, who know their subject thoroughly. You have to work hard to become a civil servant, study, pass exams, then slowly climb up the hierarchy, thereby gaining experience. The politician just jumps from being a lowly clerk, or some uneducated zamindar to become a powerful minister, lording over much more educated men. There should also be exams to become a minister, a minimum of knowledge and skills should be required of the man who says he wants to serve the nation. It matters not if he comes from a low caste, but he should have in his heart a little bit of the selflessness of the Kshatriya and a few drops of the wisdom of the Brahmin.

Nobody is saying that the caste system should be praised, for it has indeed degenerated; but it would also help in enhancing India's self-pride if Indians realised that once it constituted a unique and harmonious system. And finally, have the people who dismiss caste as an Aryan imposition on the Dravidians, or as an inhuman and nazi system, pondered the fact that it is no worse than the huge class differences you can see nowadays in South America, or even in the United States, where many Negroes live below the poverty level? And can you really exclude it off-hand, when it still survives so much in the villages - and even in more educated circles, where one still marries in matching castes, with the help of an astrologer? Does the caste system need to be transformed, to recapture its old meaning and once more incarnate a spiritual hierarchy of beings? Or has it to be recast in a different mould, taking into account the parameters of modern Indian society? Or else, will it finally disappear altogether from India, because it has become totally irrelevant today ? At any rate, Hindus should not allow this factor to be exploited shamelessly against them, as it has been in the last two centuries, by missionaries, "secular" historians, Muslims, and by pre and post-independence Indian politicians - each for their own purpose.

Thus, once these three disinformations, that of the Aryans, the Vedas and the caste system, have been set right, one can begin to understand in its proper perspective the Wonder that WAS India.

Chapter 5

The greatness of ancient India

The Vedas form the foundation stone of a prodigious civilisation which has no equal in the world. Yet, many western historians have often described India ONLY as a cultural, social, or spiritual wonder. For some other historians, such France's Jacques Dupuis, there was even a "barbaric spirit" alive in ancient India: "it is obvious that the religion of rites which characterises the cults of the Vedic epoch never reached the level of what we in the West call "ethics"... Yet, the Hindu mind of Vedic times had focussed its genius on ALL apects of human life, from the most material, to the highest spiritual, as Sri Aurobindo points out: "The tendency of the West is to live from below upward and from out inward... The inner existence is thus formed and governed by external powers. India's constant aim has been on the contrary, to find a basis of living in the higher spiritual truth and to live from the inner spirit outwards". (India's Rebirth, 109). The old Vedic seers said the same thing in a different form: "their divine foundation was above even while they stood below. Let its rays be settled deep within us."

The foundations of Indian society were thus unique, because all aspects of life were turned towards the spiritual. The original social system was divided in four "varnas", or four castes, which corresponded to each one's inner capacities. In turn, the life of a man was separated in four ashramas.

That of the student, the householder, the recluse and the yogi. The elders taught the student that "the true aim of life is to find your soul". The teaching was always on the guru-chelas principle, and the teacher being considered a representative of God, got profound respect and obedience from his pupils. Everything was taught to the students: art, literature, polity, the science of war, the development of the body -all this far away from the cities, in an environment of nature, conducive to inner growth, which was ecological, long before it became imperative and fashionable.

Indian society of that time was neither dry nor ascetic: it satisfied the urges, desires and needs of its ordinary people, particularly of the husband and wife - the beauty and comfort of Mohenjo-Daro is testimony to that fact. It taught them that perfection could be attained in all spheres of life, even in the art of physical love, where Indians excelled, as vouched so powerfully and artistically by Khajurao and the Kama-sutra.

And when man had satisfied his external being, when he had paid his debt to society and grown into wisdom, it was time to discover the spirit and roam the width and breadth of India, which at that period was covered by forests. In time he would become a yogi, young disciples would gather around him and he would begin imparting all the knowledge, worldly and inner, gathered in a lifetime and the cycle would thus start again. That the great majority did not go beyond the first two stages is no matter; this is the very reason why Indian society provided the system of castes, so that each one fitted in the mould his inner development warranted.

"It is on this firm and noble basis that Indian civilisation grew to maturity and became rich and splendid and unique," writes Sri Aurobindo." It lived with a noble, ample and vigorous order and freedom; it developed a great literature, sciences, arts, crafts, industries; it rose to the highest possible ideals of knowledge and culture, of arduous greatness and heroism,

The greatness of ancient India

of kindness, philanthropy and human sympathy and oneness. It laid the inspired basis of wonderful spiritual philosophies; it examined the secret of external nature and discovered and lived the boundless and miraculous truths of the inner being; it fathomed self and understood and possessed the world"... (Foundations of Indian Culture, p.116-117)

How far we are from some western Indologists' vision of a militant Hinduism and evil Aryans, however brilliant the social and artistic civilisation he describes! For not only did the Hindus (not the Indians, but the Hindus), demonstrate their greatness in all fields of life, social, artistic, spiritual, but they had also developed a wonderful political system.

A unique polity

Another of these great prejudices with which Indians had to battle for centuries, is that whatever the spiritual, cultural, artistic, even social greatness of India, it always was disunited, except under Ashoka and some of the Mughal emperors -just a bunch of barbarian rulers, constantly fighting amongst themselves -and that it was thanks to the Mughals and the British, that India was finally politically united. This is doing again a grave injustice to India. The Vedic sages had devised a monarchical system, whereby the king was at the top, but could be constitutionally challenged. In fact, it even allowed for men's inclination to war, but made sure that it never went beyond a certain stage, for only professional armies fought and the majority of the population remained untouched. Indeed, at no time in ancient India were there great fratricidal wars, like those between the British and the French, or even the Protestants and the Catholics within France itself. Moreover, the system allowed for a great federalism: for instance, a long time after the Vedic fathers, the real power lay in the village panchayats. Sri Aurobindo refutes the charge (which Basham levels), that India has always shown an incompetence for any free and sound political organisation and has been constantly a divided nation. "There always was a strong democratic element in pre-Muslim India, which certainly showed a certain similarity with Western parliamentary forms, but these institutions were INDIAN". The early Indian system was that of the clan, or tribal system, founded upon the equality of all members of the tribe. In the same way, the village community had its own assembly, the "visah", with only the king above this democratic body. The priests, who acted as the sacrifice makers and were poets, occultists and yogis, had no other occupation in life and their positions were thus not hereditary but depended on their inner abilities. And it was the same thing with warriors, merchants, or lower class people. "Even when these classes became hereditary," remarks Sri Aurobindo, from the king downwards to the Shudra, the predominance, say of the Brahmins, did not result in a theocracy, because the Brahmins in spite of their ever-increasing and finally predominant authority, did not and could not usurp in India the political power". (Foundations of Indian Culture p. 326). The rishi had a peculiar place, he was the sage, born from any caste, who was often counsellor to the king, to whom he was also the religious preceptor.

Later it seems that it was the republican form of government which took over many parts of India. In some cases these "republics" appear to have been governed by a democratic assembly and some came out of a revolution; in other cases, they seem to have had an oligarchic senate. But they enjoyed throughout India a solid reputation for the excellence of their civil administration and the redoubtable efficiency of their armies. It is to be noted that these Indian republics existed long before the Greek ones, although the world credits the Greeks with having created democracy; but as usual history is recorded through the prism of the Western world and is very selective indeed. One should also add that none of these Indian republics developed an aggressive

The greatness of ancient India

colonising spirit and that they were content to defend themselves and forge alliances amongst themselves.

But after the invasion of Alexander's armies, India felt for the first time the need to unify its forces. Thus the monarchical system was raised-up again; but once more, there was no despotism as happened in Europe until the French revolution: the Indian king did enjoy supreme power, but he was first the representative and guardian of Dharma, the sacred law; his power was not personal and there were safeguards against abuses so that he could be removed. Furthermore, although the king was a Hindu, Hinduism was never the state religion, and each cult enjoyed its liberties. Thus could the Jews and the Parsis and the Jains and the Buddhists, and even the early Christians (who abused that freedom), practised their faith in peace. Which religion in the world can boast of such tolerance ?

As in a human being, a nation has a soul, which is eternal; and if this soul, this idea-force, is strong enough, it will keep evolving new forms to reincarnate itself constantly. "And a people," maintains Sri Aurobindo, "who learn consciously to think always in terms of Dharma, of the eternal truth behind man, and learn to look beyond transient appearances, such as the people of India, always survives" (Foundations of Indian Culture, p.334).

And in truth, Indians always regarded life as a manifestation of Self and the master idea that governed life, culture and social ideals of India has been the seeking of man for his inner self-everything was organised around this single goal. Thus, Indian politics, although very complex, always allowed a communal freedom for self-determination. In the last stages of the pre-Muslim period, the summit of the political structure was occupied by three governing bodies: the king and his Ministerial Council, the Metropolitan Assembly and the General Assembly of the kingdom. The members of the Ministerial Council were drawn from all castes. Indeed the whole Indian system was founded upon a close participation of all the classes; even the Shudra had his share in the civic life. Thus the Council had a fixed number of Brahmin, Kshatrya, Vaishya and Shudra representatives, with the Vaishya having a greater preponderance. And in turn, each town, each village, had its own metropolitan civic assembly allowing a great amount of autonomy. Even the great Ashoka was defeated in his power tussle with his Council and he had practically to abdicate.

It is this system which allowed India to flower in an unprecedented way, to excel perhaps as no other nation had done before her, in all fields, be it literature, architecture, sculpture, or painting and develop great civilisations, one upon the other and one upon the other, each one more sumptuous, more grandiose, more glittering than the previous one.

A wonderful literature

Some of the critics of Sanskrit literature feel that " it is dry and monotonous, or can only be appreciated after a considerable effort of the imagination" , which shows a total misunderstanding of the greatness of the genius of that "mother of all languages". Sri Aurobindo evidently disagrees with that opinion : "the ancient and classical literature of the Sanskrit tongue shows both in quality and in body an abundance of excellence, in their potent originality and force and beauty, in their substance and art and structure, in grandeur and justice and charm of speech, and in the heightened width of the reach of their spirit which stands very evidently in the front rank among the world's great literatures." (Foundations of Indian Culture p. 255).

Four masterpieces seem to embody India's genius in literature: the Vedas, the Upanishads, the Ramayana, the Mahabharata. As seen earlier, the Vedas represent "a creation of an early and intuitive and symbolic mentality" (Foundations of Indian Culture, p.260). It was only because the Vedic rishis were careful to clothe their spiritual experiences in symbols, so that only the initiated would grasp them, that their meaning has escaped us, particularly after they were translated in the last two centuries. "The Veda is the WORD discovering truth and clothing in image and symbol, the mystic significance of life", wrote Sri Aurobindo. (India's Rebirth, p.95)

As to the Upanishads, asserts the sage from Pondichery, "they are the supreme work of the Indian mind, that of the highest self-expression of genius, its sublimest poetry, its greatest creation of the thought and word... a large flood of spiritual revelation." (Foundations of Indian Culture p.269). The Upanishads are philosophy, religion and poetry blended together. They record high spiritual experiences, are a treaty of intuitive philosophy and show an extraordinary poetic rhythm. It is also a book of ecstasy: an ecstasy of luminous knowledge, of fulfilled experience, "a book to express the wonder and beauty of the rarest spiritual self-vision and the profoundest illumined truth of Self and God and the Universe", writes Sri Aurobindo (Found. of Indian Culture, 269). The problem is that the translations do not render the beauty of the original text, because these masterpieces have been misunderstood by foreign translators, who only strive to bring out the intellectual meaning without grasping the soul contents of it and do not perceive the ecstasy of the seer "seeing" his experiences.

But without doubt, it is the Mahabarata and the Ramayana, which are dearest to all Indians, even today. Both the Mahabarata and the Ramayana are epical, in the spirit as well as the purpose. The Mahabarata is on a vast scale, maybe unsurpassed even today, the epic of the soul and tells a story of the ethics of India of that time, its social, political and cultural life. It is, notes Sri Aurobindo, "the expression of the mind of a nation, it is the poem of itself written by a whole nation... A vast temple unfolding slowly its immense and complex idea from chamber to chamber" (Foundations of Indian Culture, p 287). More than that even, it is the HISTORY OF DHARMA, of deva against asura, the strife between divine and titanic forces. You find on one side, a civilisation founded on Dharma, and on the other, beings who are embodiments of asuric egoism and misuse of Dharma. It is cast in the mould of tales, legends, anecdotes, telling stories of philosophical, religious, social, spiritual values: "as in Indian architecture, there is the same power to embrace great spaces in a total view and the same tendency to fill them with an abundance of minute, effective, vivid and significant detail". (Foundations of Indian Culture, p 288).

The Baghavad Gita must be the supreme work of spiritual revelation in the whole history of our human planet, for it is the most comprehensive, the most revealing, the highest in its intuitive reach. No religious book ever succeeded to say nearly everything that needs to be known on the mysteries of human life: why death, why life, why suffering? Why fighting, why duty? Dharma, the supreme law, the duty to one's soul, the adherence to truth, the faithfulness to the one and only divine reality which pertains to all things in matter and spirit. "Such then is the divine Teacher of the Gita, the eternal Avatar, the Divine who has descended into human consciousness, the Lord seated within the heart of all beings, He who guides from behind the veil all our thought and action". (Sri Aurobindo; Essays on the Gita, page 17).

Many scholars have also seen in Krishna's discourse to Arjuna, when the latter throws down his bow and says: " I- will- not- fight", an exhortation not to a physical war, but to an inner war, against one's own ego and weaknesses. While there is no doubt that the Bhagavad Gita is essentially a divine message of yoga – that is of transforming one's own nature while reaching towards the Absolute - it is also fundamental to understand that it uniquely reconciles war with the notion of duty, dharma.

Since the beginning of time, war has been an integral part of man's quest. Yet, it is the most misunderstood factor of our human history. And that is but natural, because, as writes Sri Aurobindo in his remarkable 'Essays on the Gita': "Man's natural tendency is to worship Nature as love and life and beauty and good and to turn away from her grim mask of death". Thus, war has often baffled or even repelled man. We saw how Ashoka turned Buddhist after the battle of Kalinga, or in the previous century how some of the American youth refused to participate in the Vietnam war; and we are witnessing today massive protests against the atom bomb.

Yet, what does the Gita say ? That sometimes, when all other means have failed and it is necessary to protect one's borders, wives, children and culture, war can become dharma. That war is a universal principle of our life, because as says Sri Aurobindo "it is evident that the actual life of man can make no real step forward without a struggle between what exists and lives and what seeks to exist". And that humanity periodically experiences in its history times in which great forces clash together for a huge destruction, and reconstruction, intellectual, social, moral, religious, political.

The Gita also stresses that there exists a struggle between righteousness and unrighteousness, between the self affirming law of Good and the forces that oppose its progression. Its message is therefore addressed to those whose duty in life is that of protecting those who are at the mercy of the strong and the violent. "It is only a few religions", writes Sri Aurobindo, "which have had the courage, like the Indian, to lift-up the image of the force that acts in the world in the figure not only of the beneficent Durga, but also of the terrible Kali in her blood-stained dance of destruction". And it is significant that this religion, Hinduism, which had this unflinching honesty and tremendous courage, has succeeded in creating a profound and widespread spirituality such as no other can parallel.

Has India understood this great nationalist message of the Gita ? Yes and no. On the one hand you have had Rajputs, Mahrattas, and Sikhs; you have had a Shivaji, a Rani of Jhansi, or a Sri Aurobindo, who, let us remember, gave a call as early as 1906 for the eviction of the British – by force if need be – at a time when the Congress was not even considering Independence. But on the other hand, apart from these few heroes, the greater mass of India seems to have been for centuries the unresisting prey of invaders. Wave after wave of Muslims intruders were able to loot, rape, kill, raze temples and govern India, because Hindu chieftains kept betraying each other and no national uprising occurred against them; the British got India for a song, bled it dry (20 millions Indians died of famine during British rule), because, except for the Great (misguided) Mutiny, there was no wave of nationalism opposed to them until very late; we also saw how in 1962 the Indian army was routed and humiliated by the Chinese, because Nehru had refused to heed the warnings posed by the Chinese. Recently, we witnessed how India reacted during the hijack of the IC flight from Kathmandu: instead of storming the plane when it was in Amritsar, India's leaders got cowed down by the prospect of human casualties from their own side and surrendered to terrorism. But in the process India's image and self-esteem suffered and the liberated separatists are now spitting even more venom and terror.

Why is this great nationalistic message of the Gita forgotten ? There are two main factors. The first one is Buddhism and the second is the philosophy of Mahatma Gandhi. Buddhism, because it made of non-violence an uncompromising, inflexible dogma, was literally wiped-off the face of India in a few centuries, as it refused to oppose any

The greatness of ancient India

resistance. It is also true that Buddhist thought indirectly influenced Hinduism as well as great contemporary figures such as Mahatma Gandhi, whose sincere but rigid adherence to non-violence may have indirectly precipitated Partition. Today, well-meaning "secular" Indian intellectuals still borrow from the Buddhist and Gandhian creed of non-violence to demonstrate why India should not have the bomb...and get wiped-out by Pakistan or China, who have no such qualms.

There is a lining in the sky, though: the Kargil war has shown that Hindu, Muslim and Christian soldiers can put their country above their religion and fight along side each other. We see today a new wave of nationalism rising not only in India, but also amongst the very influential expatriate Indian community, particularly in the US. The nationalist message of the Gita is not only still relevant today, but it is essential for India's survival in the face of so many threats: the "Islamic" bomb of Pakistan, the hegemonic tendencies of China, or the globalisation and westernisation of India, which is another form of war. One would be tempted thus to address this message to this wonderful, diverse, and extraordinary country, which has survived so many threats during her eight thousand years history: ARISE AGAIN O INDIA AND REMEMBER KRISHNA'S MESSAGE TO ARJUNA : TRUTH IS THE FOUNDATION OF REAL SPIRITUALITY AND COURAGE ITS SOUL.

The Ramayana's inner genius does not differ from the Mahabharata's, except by a greater simplicity of plan, a finer glow of poetry maybe. It seems to have been written by a single hand, as there is no deviation from story to story... But it is, remarks Sri Aurobindo, "like a vastness of vision, an even more winged-flight of epic in the conception and sustained richness of minute execution in the detail (289)." For Indians, the Ramayana embodies the highest and most cherished ideals of manhood, beauty, courage, purity, gentleness. The subject is the same as in the Mahabharata: the struggle between the forces of light and darkness; but the setting is more imaginative, supernatural and there is an intensification of the characters in both their goodness and evil. As in the Mahabharata too, we are shown the ideal man with his virtues of courage, selflessness, virtue and spiritualised mind. The asuric forces have a near cosmic dimension of super-human egoism and near divine violence, as the chaste angels of the Bible possessed after them. "The poet makes us conscious of the immense forces that are behind our life and sets his action in a magnificent epic scenery." We may too mention Kalidasa, whose poetry was imitated by all succeeding generations of poets, who tried to copy the perfect and harmoniously designed model of his poetry. The Puranas and the Tantras, "which contain in themselves", writes Sri Aurobindo, "the highest spiritual and philosophical truths, while embodying them in forms that are able to carry something of them to the popular imagination and feeling by way of legend, tale, symbols, miracles and parables" (Found of Indian Culture P.312). The Vaishnava poetry, which sings the cry of the soul for God, as incarnated by the love stories of Radha and Krishna, which have struck forever Indian popular imagination, because they symbolise the nature in man seeking for the Divine soul through love. Valmiki also moulded the Indian mind with his depiction of Rama and Sita, another classic of India's love couples and one that has survived through the myth of enduring worship, in the folklore of this country, along with the popular figures of Hanuman and Lakshman. "His diction", remarks Sri Aurobindo, "is shaped in the manner of the direct intuitive mind as earlier expressed in the Upanishads".

But Indian literature is not limited to Sanskrit or Pali. In Tamil, Tiruvalluvar wrote the highest ever gnomic poetry, perfect in its geometry, plan and force of execution. In Hindi, Tulsidas is a master of lyric intensity and the sublimity of epic imagination. In Marathi, Ramdas, poet, thinker, yogi, deals with the birth and awakening of a whole nation, with all the charm and the strength of a true bhakti. In Bengal, there is Kashiram, who retold in simple manner the Mahabharata and the Ramayana, accompanied by Tulsidas who did the same thing in Hindi and who managed to combine lyric intensity, romantic flight of imagination, while retaining the original sublimity of the story. One cannot end this short retrospective without mentioning Chaitanya, Nanak, Kabir, Mirabai...All these remarkable writers have often baffled the Western mind, which could never understand the greatness of Indian literature, forgetting that in India everything was centred around the spiritual.

A spiritualised Indian art

"The highest business of Indian art has always been to describe something of the Self, of the soul, contrary to Western art, which either harps at the superficially beautiful or dwells at the vital-unconscious level." (Sri Aurobindo. Foundations of Indian Culture p.208).

This is indeed the great difference between Indian art and other art forms. For the Indian artist first visualises in his inner being the truth of the element he wants to express and creates it in his intuitive mind, before externalising it. Stories of how Indian sculptors of ancient times used to meditate for one year before starting on their particular work, are common. Not the idea of the intellect or mental imagination, but the essence, the emotion, the spirit. Thus, for the Indian artist, material forms, colour, line, design, are only physical means of expression, NOT his first preoccupation. So he will not attempt, as in Western art, which in its heyday continuously recreated scenes of Christ's life or that of saints, to reconstitute some scene of Buddha's life, but instead, he will endeavor to REVEAL the calm of Nirvana. And every accessory is an aid, a MEANS to do so, "for here spirit carries the form, while in western art, form carries whatever they think is spirit".(Foundations p.211).

In effect, Indian art, its architecture for instance, demands an inner eye to be appreciated, otherwise its truth will not reveal itself. Great temples in India are an architectural expression of an ancient spiritual culture. Its many varied forms express the manifestation of the infinite multiplicity which fills the oneness of India. And indeed even the Moslem architecture was taken up by India's creative genius and transformed into something completely Indian.

Indian sculpture also springs from spiritual insight and it is unique by its total absence of ego. Very few of India's sculptural masterpieces are signed, for instance; they are rather the work of a collective genius whose signature could be "INDIA". "Most ancient sculptures of India embody in visible form what the Upanishads threw out into inspired thought and the Mahabaratha and the Ramayana portrayed by the word in life", observes Sri Aurobindo. (Foundations, p.230). The Gods of Indian sculpture are cosmic beings, embodiments of some great spiritual power. And every movement, hands, eyes, posture, conveys an INNER meaning, as in the Natarajas, for example. Sri Aurobindo admired particularly the Kalasanhara Shiva, about which he said: "it is supreme, not only by the majesty, power, calmly forceful controlled dignity and kinship of existence which the whole spirit and pose visibly incarnates...but much more by the concentrated divine passion of the spiritual overcoming of time and existence which the artist has succeeded in putting into eye and brow and mouth..." (Foundations P.233).

Indian painting has, unfortunately, been largely erased by time, as in the case of the Ajanta caves. It even went through an eclipse and was revived by the Mughal influence. But what remains of Indian paintings show the immensity of the work and the genius of it. The paintings that have mostly survived from ancient times are those of the Buddhist artists; but painting in India was certainly pre-Buddhist. Indeed in ancient India, there were six "limbs", six essential elements, "sadanga" to a great painting. The first is "rupabheda", distinction of forms; the second is "pramana", arrangement of lines; the third is "bhava", emotion of aesthetic feelings; the fourth is "lavanya", seeking for beauty; the fifth is "sadrsya", truth of the form; and the sixth is "varnikashanga", harmony of colours. Western art always flouts the first principle "rupabheda", the universal law of the right distinction of forms, for it constantly strays into intellectual or fantasy extravagances which belong to the intermediate world of sheer fantasia. On the other hand, in the Indian paintings, Sri Aurobindo remarks that : "the Indian artist sets out from the other end of the scale of values of experience which connect life and the spirit. The whole creative force here comes from a spiritual and psychic vision, the emphasis of the physical is secondary and always deliberately limited so as to give an overwhelmingly spiritual and psychic impression and everything is suppressed which does not serve this purpose". (Foundations, p.246). It is unfortunate that today most Indian painting imitates Western modern art, but for a few exceptions. And it is hoped that Indian painters will soon come back to the essential, which is the vision of the inner eye, the transcription, not of the religious, but of the spiritual and the occult.

India's ancient civilisations

It is upon this great and lasting foundations, cultural, artistic, social and political, that India, Mother India, Sanatana Dharma, produced many wonderful periods. We are not here to make an historical review of them; a few of their glorious names will suffice, for with them still rings the splendour and towering strength of the eternal spirit of the Vedic fathers...

The Kashi kingdom of Benares, which was founded upon the cult of Shiva and was the spiritual and cultural capital of India, was, we are told, a great show of refinement and beauty, and that at least ten centuries before Christ was born, according to conservative estimates. Remember that Gautama the Buddha preached his first sermon in the suburbs of Benares at Sarnath. "Kashi", eulogises Alain Danielou, "was a kind of Babylon, a sacred city , a centre of learning, of art and pleasures, the heart of Indian civilisation, whose origins were lost in prehistoric India and its kings ruled over a greater part of northern and even southern India".

We may also mention the Gandhara kingdom, which included Peshawar, parts of Afghanistan, Kashmir and was thus protecting India from invasions,as Sri Aurobindo points out: "the historic weakness of the Indian peninsula has always been until modern times its vulnerability through the North-western passes. This weakness did not exist as long as ancient India extended northward far beyond the Indus and the powerful kingdoms of Gandhara and Vahlika presented a firm bulwark against foreign invasion". (Found. 373).

But soon these kingdoms collapsed and Alexander's armies marched into India, the first foreign invasion of the country, if one discounts the Aryan theory. Henceforth, all the theorists and politicians thought about the unifying of India and this heralded the coming of the first great Emperor: Chandra Gupta, who vanquished the remnants of Alexander's armies and assimilated some of the Greek civilisation's great traits. Thus started the mighty Mauryan empire, which represents the first effort at unifying India politically. A little of that time is known through the Arthashastra of Kautilya, or Chanakya, Minister of Chandragupta, who gives us glimpses of the conditions and state organisation of that time. Chandragupta, who was the founder of the Maurya dynasty, came from a low caste, liberated Punjab from the Greeks and managed to conquer the whole of the Indian subcontinent

The greatness of ancient India

except for the extreme South. The administrative set-up of Chandragupta was so efficient that later the Muslims and the English retained it, only bringing here and there a few superficial modifications. Chandragupta in true Indian tradition renounced the world during his last years and lived as an anchorite at the feet of the Jain saint Bhadrabahu in Shravanabelagola, near Mysore. Historians, such as Alain Danielou, label Chanakya and Chandragupta's rule as Machiavellian: "It was", writes Danielou, "a centralised despotism, resting on military power and disguised into a constitutional monarchy". (Histoire de l'Inde p. 114). This again is a very westernised view of post-vedic India, which cannot conceive that Hindustan could have devised a constitutional monarchy before the Europeans.

And Sri Aurobindo obviously disagrees: "The history of this empire, its remarkable organisation, administration, public works, opulence, magnificent culture and the vigour, the brilliance, the splendid fruitfulness of life of the peninsula under its shelter, ranks among the greatest constructed and maintained by the genius of earth's great peoples. India has no reason, from this point of view, to be anything but proud of her ancient achievement in empire-building or to surrender to the hasty verdict that denies to her antique civilisation a strong practical genius or high political virtue" (Found. 373).

In the South, the Andhras were dominating from Cape Comorin to the doors of Bombay. Then came the Pallavas, who were certainly one of the most remarkable dynasties of medieval India. The first Pallavas appeared near Kanchi in the 3rd century, but it is only with King Simhavishnu that they reached their peak. Simhavishnu conquered the Chera, the Cholas, the Pandya dynasties of the South and annexed Ceylon. It is to this period that belong the magnificent frescoes of Mahabalipuram which have survived until today. During the Pallavas' rule, great cities such as Kanchi flourished, busy ports like Mahabalipuram sprang-up, and art blossomed under all its forms. So did the Sanskrit language, which went through a great revival period and the Dravidian architecture style of Southern India, famous for its mandapams, which has passed down, from generation to generation until today. The Bhakti movement also developed in South India during the Pallavas and it gave a new orientation to Hinduism.

At the same time, the dynasty of the Vardhamana was establishing its might in the centre of India. Founded by King Pushyabhuti, « who had acquired great spiritual powers by the practice of Shivaite tantrism", writes Jean Danielou, it reached its peak under King Harsha, who, starting with Bengal and Orissa, conquered what is today UP, Bihar, extending his empire northwards towards Nepal and Kashmir and southwards to the Narmada river. Alain Danielou feels "that King Harsha symbolised all that was right in Hindu monarchy, wielding an absolute power, but each sphere of administration was enjoying a large autonomy and the villages were functioning like small republics". The Chinese traveller, Hiuen Tsang, another admirer of Harsha, writes that he was an untiring man, just and courageous, constantly surveying all parts of his kingdom.

India's influence was then at its highest, her culture and religions expanded all the way to Burma, Cambodia, Siam, Ceylon and in the other direction to Mecca, where Shiva's black lingam was revered by Arabians.

But in 632, a few years before the death of King Harsha, started the bloody history of Muslim invasions in overtaking India, unparalleled in the whole of world history, for its sheer horror and terror.

Chapter 6

Islam And India

Muslim invasions are still today a very controversial subject, since Indian history books have chosen to keep quiet about this huge chunk of Indian history - nearly 10 centuries of horrors. At Independence, Nehru too, put it aside, perhaps because he thought that this was a topic which could divide India, as there was a strong Muslim minority which chose to stay and not emigrate to Pakistan. Yet, nothing has marked India's psyche - or the Hindu silent majority, if you wish - as much as the Muslim invasions. And whatever happens in contemporary India, is a consequence of these invasions, whether it is the creation of Godhra or Pakistan, whether it is Kashmir, whether it is Ayodhya, or Kargil. There is no point in passing a moral judgment on these invasions, as they are a thing of the past. Islam is one of the world's youngest religions, whose dynamism is not in question; unfortunately it is a militant religion, as it believes that there is only one God and all other Gods are false. And so as long as this concept is ingrained in the minds of Muslims, there will be a problem of tolerance, of tolerating other creeds. And this is what happened in India from the 7th century onwards : invaders, who believed in one God, came upon this country which had a million gods... And for them it was the symbol of all what they thought was wrong. So the genocide - and the word genocide has to be used - which was perpetrated was tremendous, because of the staunch resistance of the 4000 year old Hindu faith. Indeed, the Muslim policy vis à vis India seems to have been a conscious and systematic destruction of everything that was beautiful, holy, refined. Entire cities were burnt down and their populations massacred. Each successive campaign brought hundreds of thousands of victims and similar numbers were deported as slaves. Every new invader often made literally his hill of Hindu skulls. Thus the conquest of Afghanistan in the year 1000, was followed by the annihilation of the entire Hindu population there; indeed, the region is still called Hindu Kush, 'Hindu slaughter'. The Bahmani sultans in central India, made it a rule to kill 100,000 Hindus a year. In 1399, Teimur killed 100,000 Hindus in a single day, and many more on other occasions. Historian Konraad Elst, in his book "Negationism in India", quotes Professor K.S. Lal, who calculated that the Hindu population decreased by eighty million between the year 1000 and 1525, indeed, probably the biggest holocaust in the world's history, far greater than the genocide of the Incas in South America by the Spanish and the Portuguese.

Regrettably, there was a conspiracy by the British, and later by India's Marxist intelligentsia to negate this holocaust. Thus, Indian students since the early twenties were taught that that there never was a Muslim genocide on the person of Hindus, but rather that the Mughals brought great refinement to Indian culture. In "Communalism and the writing of Indian history", for instance, Romila Thapar, Harbans Mukhia and Bipan Chandra, professors at the JNU in New Delhi, the Mecca of secularism and negationism in India, denied the Muslim genocide by replacing it instead with a conflict of classes :

"Muslims brought the notion of egalitarianism in India", they argue. The redoubtable Romila Thapar in her "Penguin History of India", co-authored with Percival Spear, writes again: "Aurangzeb's supposed intolerance, is little more than a hostile legend based on isolated acts such as the erection of a mosque on a temple site in Benares".

What are the facts, according to Muslim records?

Aurangzeb (1658-1707) did not just build an isolated mosque on a destroyed temple, he ordered all temples destroyed and mosques to be built on their sites. Among them the Kashi Vishvanath, one of the most sacred places of Hindu worship, Krishna's birth temple in Mathura, the rebuilt Somnath temple on the coast of Gujurat, the Vishnu temple replaced with the Alamgir mosque now overlooking Benares and the Treta-ka-Thakur temple in Ayodhya. The number of temples destroyed by Aurangzeb is counted in five, if not six figures, according to his own official court chronicles: "Aurangzeb ordered all provincial governors to destroy all schools and temples of the pagans and to make a complete end to all pagan teachings and practices"... "Hasan Ali Khan came and said that 172 temples in the area had been destroyed"... "His majesty went to Chittor and 63 temples were destroyed"... "Abu Tarab, appointed to destroy the idol-temples of Amber, reported that 66 temples had been razed to the ground". Aurangzeb did not stop at destroying temples, their users were also wiped-out; even his own brother, Dara Shikoh, was executed for taking an interest in Hindu religion and the Sikh Guru Teg Bahadur was beheaded because he objected to Aurangzeb's forced conversions.

This genocide is still a reality which should not be wished away. Because what the Muslims invasions have done to India is to instil terror in the Hindu collective psyche, which still lingers many centuries later and triggers unconscious reactions. The paranoia displayed today by Indians, their indiscipline, their lack of charity for their own brethren, the abject disregard of their environment, are a direct consequence of these invasions. What India has to do today, is to look squarely at the facts pertaining to these invasions and come to terms with them, without any spirit of vengeance, so as to regain a little bit of self-pride. It would also help the Muslim community of India to acknowledge these horrors, which paradoxically, were committed against them, as they are the

Hindus who were then converted by force, their women raped, their children taken into slavery – even though today they have made theirs the religion which their ancestors once hated.

Chapter 7

The Ugly European Colonisers

No country in the world has shown as much tolerance as India, by accepting in its fold persecuted religious minorities from all over the planet. Take the Jews, for instance, who have been persecuted and treated as second-class citizens everywhere after fleeing the destruction of the temple of Jerusalem. In India, not only were they welcomed, but also they were allowed to live and practise their religion peacefully, till most of them went back to Israel after Independence. But it is not only the Jews, but also the Parsis, who fled persecution by the Muslims in Iran, or the Christian Syrians, who first landed in India in the 3rd century, or the Arab merchants who from time immemorial were allowed to establish trading posts in Kerala. Or even the Jesuits, who were welcomed when they landed with Vasco de Gama in Calicut in 1495. But, like many others, they quickly turned against their benefactors and set out not only to exploit India commercially, but also attempted to impose their own religions on the "heathens", the pagans, the infidels.

It is thus a bit of a paradox when one hears today Indian intellectuals claim that Hindus are intolerant, fanatic, or "fundamentalists". Because in the whole history of India, Hindus have not only shown that they are extremely tolerant, but Hinduism is probably the only religion in the world which never tried to convert others – forget about conquering other countries to propagate its own religion.

This is not true with Christianity, it is not true with Islam - it is not even true with Buddhism, as Buddhists had missionaries who went all over Asia and converted people. This historical tolerance of Hinduism is never taken into account by foreign correspondents covering India and even by Indian journalists. If it was, Indians might at least take some pride in their country's boundless generosity towards others... Indians have a very short memory of themselves, maybe because they never cared to write down their own history.

Thus, this beautiful tolerance was taken advantage of by numerous invaders – particularly European colonisers. The Portuguese for instance, were allowed to establish trading posts in the 15th century by the Zamorin of Cochin. And what did they do? Alfonso de Albuquerque started a reign of terror in Goa, razing temples to erect churches in their stead, burning "heretics", crucifying Brahmins, using false theories to forcibly convert the lower castes and encouraging his soldiers to take Indian mistresses. Later, the British missionaries in India were always supporters of colonialism; they encouraged it and their whole structure was based on "the good Western civilised world being brought to the pagans". In the words of Claudius Buchanan, a chaplain attached to the East India Company: "Neither truth, nor honesty, honour, gratitude, nor charity, is to be found in the breast of a Hindoo" What a comment about a nation that gave the world the Vedas and the Upanishads ! After the failed mutiny of 1857, the missionaries became even more militant, using the secular arm of the British Raj, who felt that the use of the sword at the service of the Gospel, was now entirely justified, so that at Independence, entire regions of the north-east were converted to Christianity. Remember how Swami Vivekananda cried in anguish at the Parliament of Religions in Chicago: "if we Hindus dig out all the dirt from the bottom of the Pacific Ocean and throw it in your faces, it will be but a speck compared to what the missionaries have done to our religion and culture."

The Ugly European Colonisers

In the late nineties, after the BJP came to power, Indian Christians complained about persecutions by Hindu "zealots". It is true that there happened two or three crimes, particularly a ghastly murder against an Australian missionary and his two young sons. But the massive outcry it evoked in the Indian Press showed clearly how Indians are constantly denying themselves and consider the life of a White Man infinitely more important and dear than the lives of a hundred Indians. Or to put it differently: the life of a Christian seems to them more sacred than the lives of many Hindus, which shows how the White Man's presence in India still has such an impact. Because when Hindus were slaughtered, whether in Punjab in the eighties, or in Kashmir in the nineties, when militants would stop buses and kill all the Hindus - men, women and children - when the last few courageous Hindus who dared to remain in Kashmir were savagely slaughtered in a village, very few voices were raised in the Indian Press - at least there never was such an outrage as provoked by the murder of the Australian missionary.

At long last, Hindus are beginning to realise the harm done by missionaries to their social and cultural fabric. Yet even today, one still hears of covert attempts at conversion by Christian missionaries. In the poor districts of Kerala for example, missionaries still use the "miracle" ploy to convert people: the naive drops a "wish" in a box placed at the entrance of the church. And lo, this wish - a loan, some cloths, a boat - is miraculously granted a few days later. Needless to say that the happy innocent converts quickly, bringing along his whole family. It is also this meekness of the Hindus towards the Christians, as if the British missionaries had permanently left an imprint of inferiority in the collective psyche of Indians, which contributes towards India's self-denial. And let us not forget that Pope John Paul II proclaimed that Asia will be the target of evangelisation in the Third Millennium: it's already happening, as according to official reports, there is a phenomenal growth of Christianity amongst the tribes of the North-East, particularly in Arunachal Pradesh.

Macaulay's Children

When they took over India, the British set about establishing an intermediary race of Indians, whom they could entrust with their work at the middle level echelons and who could one day be convenient instruments to rule by proxy, or semi-proxy. The tool to shape these "British clones" was education. In the words of Macaulay, the "pope" of British schooling in India: "We must at present do our best to form a class, who may be interpreters between us and the millions we govern; a class of persons, Indians in blood and colour, but English in taste, in opinions, in morals and in intellects." Macaulay had very little regard for Hindu culture and education: "all the historical information which can be collected from all the books which have been written in the Sanskrit language, is less valuable than what may be found in the most paltry abridgement used at preparatory schools in England". Or: "Hindus have a literature of small intrinsic value, hardly reconcilable with morality, full of monstrous superstitions".

It seems today that India's Marxist and Muslim intelligentsia could not agree more with Macaulay, for his dream has come true: the greatest adversaries of an "Indianised and spiritualised education" are the descendants of these "Brown Sahibs": the "secular" politicians, the journalists, the top bureaucrats, in fact the whole westernised cream of India. And what is even more paradoxical, is that most of them are Hindus !

The recent Sabamarti burning followed by the rioting in Gujurat, showed again how Indian journalists are true descendants of Macaulay. Here you had fifty eight innocent Hindus, the majority of them being women and children, burnt in the most horrible manner, for no other crime but the fact that they want to build a temple dedicated to the most cherished of Hindu Gods, Ram, on a site which has been held sacred by Hindus for thousands of years. When a Graham Staines is burnt alive, all of India's English press goes overboard in condemning his killers, but when 58 Graham Staines are murdered, they report it without comment. No doubt, the rioting which followed in Gurjurat against the Muslims is equally unpardonable. No doubt, Indian and foreign journalists who rushed to Gujurat, wrote sincerely: after all they saw innocent women, children, men, being burnt, killed, raped. Which decent journalist, who has at heart the reporting of truth would not cry out against such a shame? But then history has shown us that no event should be taken out of context, and that there is in India, amongst the Hindu majority, a simmering anger against Muslims, who have terribly persecuted the Hindus and yet manage to make it look as if they are the persecuted.

And once again, the western press coverage of the Gujurat rioting comes back to haunt India: Hindus targeting Muslims, fundamentalism against innocence, minority being persecuted by majority. But when will the true India be sincerely portrayed by its own journalists, so that the western press can be positively influenced?

The Impoverishment of India

India is always associated in the world with poverty : Mother Teresa, Unicef, or Calcutta. This image has been enhanced by books such as the City of Joy, an international best-seller, which takes a little part of India - the Calcutta slums - and gives the impression to the naïve and ignorant western readers, that it constitutes the whole of India. Another factor which reinforces the image of poverty is the tremendous fame which Mother Theresa enjoyed in her lifetime - and even after her death, as she is in the process of being made a saint. While it is true that Mother Theresa did a tremendous job in Calcutta, she never tried to counterbalance the very negative image of India that her name was carrying, with some praise for the country which had adopted her for fifty years. She could have spoken for instance about the great hospitality of Indians, or the open-mindedness of the Hindu religion, which had allowed her to practise Christianity near one of the most sacred temples of the country, or even about the near worship which most Hindus showed for her.

It is true that there is a tremendous amount of poverty in India, and that many people can only afford one meal a day. But four things should be known. Firstly, that until the 18th century, in spite of the repeated Muslim invasions, India was known as one of the richest countries of the world, the land "of milk and honey". You only have to read the numerous accounts of travellers from different countries, who all marvelled at India's prosperity.

The second thing, is that all the great famines of India happened during the British time. Many historians, such as Frenchman Guy Deleury, have documented the economic rape of India by the British : "Industrially the British suffocated India , gradually strangling Indian industries whose finished products, textiles in particular, were of a quality unique in the world which has made them famous over the centuries. Instead they oriented Indian industries towards jute, cotton, tea, oil seeds, which they needed as raw materials for their home industries. They employed cheap labour for the enterprises while traditional artisans were perishing. India, which used to be a land of plenty, where milk and honey flowed, started drying" (Modèle Indou). According to British records, one million Indians died of famine between 1800 and 1825, 4 million between 1825-1850, 5 million between 1850-1875 and 15 million between 1875-1900. Thus 25 million Indians died in 100 years ! The British must be proud of their bloody record. It is probably more honourable and straightforward to kill in the name of Allah, than in the guise of petty commercial interests and total disregard for the ways of a 5000 year civilisation. Thus, by the beginning of the 20th century, India was bled dry and there were no resources left.

The third fact, is that after Independence, whatever poverty there still was in this country, there were no more famines, as India managed to become self-sufficient in food through the Green Revolution (whatever negative side effects it had on India's ecology - but that is another story). This is a great achievement, a tremendous task of which India can be proud. For if you look at China, India's largest neighbour, which always invites natural comparison with India as they share many of the same problems and characteristics, it went through tremendous traumas after independence. Millions died of hunger, for instance, when Mao diverted peasants from cultivating the land, in his misguided and megalomaniac effort to increase steel production.

Finally, the history of the British would be incomplete without mentioning the positive side. The unification of India by a single language, although it is hoped that it will be eventually replaced by India's true language of the future, acceptable to all. The vast railway system, which more than anything else unified India. The remarkable Postal system, whose structures have survived till today. The roads network of India. But all these were not really meant for the welfare of India, but for a better administration of their own colony.

And ultimately, the question should be asked: "did the British leave India with any understanding, any inkling of the greatness of the country they had lived with for two centuries"? Except for a few souls like Annie Besant or Sister Nivedita, the answer seems to be: NO. And today's British Prime Minister probably does not understand one bit more about India than Lord Mountbatten did. But then Mountabatten ought to have known better.

Chapter 8

Swaraj

Which Indian children of today know that Sri Aurobindo was one of the early revolutionaries advocating India's independence, when the Congress was still only preaching constitutional agitation? India seems to have forgotten that most of the linguistic, archaeological and historic theories on which India's supposed history and datings are based, were devised by early historians, like Jones or Max Mueller (who has been forgotten in the West but is treated like an icon in India) who were at the service of the British Government. And naturally, as we have seen earlier the British wanted a history of India that suited their designs and showed Indians as an inferior race, who inherited their superior realisations, like the Vedas, from a western-aryan influence, or its mathematics from Alexander the Great. Therefore the theory of the Aryan invasion, the voluntary post-dating of the Vedas (by Max Mueller himself) and the decrying of the caste system. Of all the Indians who embraced these false myths, Nehru must be the most to blame. His love of Western civilisation (hence his infatuation for Lady Mountabatten, which, it seems, stemmed more from his fascination for the White Skin and the pomp which surrounded the Viceroys of India, than from any sexual or romantic inclination), his contempt for his own culture and the Marxisation he has effected on India, which still survives today, have done immense harm to the country.

Indian history books teach that the Independence Movement started with the Indian National Congress. But originally, the Congress was a tool fashioned by the British for their own use. Witness the fact that it all began in December 1885, with an Englishman, A.O. Hume, with the avowed aim to: "Allow all those who work for the national (read British) good to meet each other personally, to discuss and decide on the political operations to start during the year".

And certainly, till the end of the 19th century, the Congress, who regarded British rule in India as a "divine dispensation", was happy with criticising moderately the Government, while reaffirming its loyalty to the Crown and its faith in "liberalism" and the British innate sense of justice!!!

Thus for a long time, the Britishers considered favourably the Congress and sought to use it to justify their continuing occupation of India. But soon, of course, it changed into suspicion and downright hostility, as the Congress, realising its folly, turned towards constitutional agitation to obtain from the British Parliament a few laws favourable to India. And the Englishmen did hand over a few crumbs here and there, such as giving Lord Sinha (Lord Sinha indeed!) the honour of becoming the first Indian to be part of the Governor's Executive Council. So what ?

What must be understood to grasp the whole history of the Congress, is that its pre-independence leaders were anglicised, western educated Indians, whose idealism was at best a dose of liberalism peppered with a bit of socialism "British Labour style". They were the outcrop of an old British policy of forming a small westernised elite, cut off from its Indian roots, which would serve in the intermediary hierarchies of the British Raj and act as a go-between the master and the slaves. Thus, not only were these Congress leaders "moderate" (as they came to be called), partially cut-off from the reality of India, from the greatness that Was India, the soul-glory of its simple people, but because their mind worked on the pattern of their masters, they turned out to be the greatest Hindu-baiters and haters of them all, as verily their descendants, even until today, still are.

But these westernised moderate Congress leaders, found it difficult to get identified by the vast mass of India which was deeply religious. Thus they encouraged the start of "reformed" Hindu movements, such as the Arya Samaj or the Brahma Samaj, through which they could attack the old Hindu system, under the guise of transforming it, which is perfectly acceptable to all Hindus, as Hinduism has always tolerated in its fold divergent movements. It is these early Congress leaders who began the slow but insidious crushing of the Hindu society. For instance, the Congress Governments, which were installed after July 1937 in most of the provinces, encouraged everywhere the development of education modelled on the British system. And comments Danielou: "the teaching of philosophy, arts, sciences, which constituted the prestigious Indian cultural tradition, became more and more ignored and COULD ONLY SURVIVE THANKS TO THE BRAHMINS, without any help whatsoever from the State." When the first true cultural, social and political movements, which had at heart the defence of India's true heritage started taking shape, such as the much decried Hindu Mahashaba, which attempted to counterbalance the Muslim League's influence, or the even more maligned Rama Rajya Parishad, initiated by the remarkable Hindu monk Swamy Karpatri, they were ridiculed by the Congress, which used to amplify the problems of untouchability, castes, or cow worshipping, to belittle these movements, which after all, were only trying to change India from a greatness that was to a greatness to be.

"The Congress", writes Danielou, "utilised to the hilt its English speaking press to present these Hindu parties as barbaric, fanatical, ridiculous; and the British media in turn, took-up, as parrots, the cry of their Indian counterparts". (Histoire de l'Inde, p. 345). To this day, nothing has changed in India: the English-speaking press still indulges in Hindu-bashing and it is faithfully copied by the western corespondents, most of whom are totally ignorant of India and turn towards Indian intellectuals to fashion their opinions.

But this strategy was good enough to convince the British that when they left, they would have to hand over power to the "respectable" Congress (after all, we are all gentlemen), even though it constituted a tiny Westernised minority, whereas India's true Hindu majority would be deprived of their right.

The Congress did turn radical finally in 1942, when, because of Mahatma Gandhi's rigorous non-violence policy, it adopted a non-co-operation attitude towards the war effort. Thus the British declared the Congress illegal, jailed most of its leaders and embarked on a policy of heavy repression. But the truth is that those of the Congress who were imprisoned and are deified today for that fact, went there not directly for India's independence, but because Mahatma Gandhi refused to co-operate in the second world war.

So, ultimately, what was true nationalism? Who were the real revolutionaries, those who had an inner vision of what the British really represented, those who knew what was the genius of India and how it was destined to be great again? Once more, we have a wrong understanding of nationalism, because we are induced in error by the West's opinions about it. In Europe, nationalism means external revolutionary movements, revolutionaries, materialism. But India's greatness has always been her spirituality, her strength was always founded upon her Spirit's hold. Not only her Brahmins, but also her Kshatriyas, Vaishyas and Shudras even, drew their heroism from that fountain. Thus in India, the

Swaraj

nationalist movement, the REAWAKENING of India's soul, started at the source, in her Spirit.

Sri Aurobindo, the Forgotten Giant of India's Independance

Sri Aurobindo was born on the 15th of August 1872 in Calcutta, he spent his first years at Rangpur (now in Bangladesh) and at the age of five is sent to Loreto Convent school in Darjeeling. His father, who wants him to have a thorough Western education, packs him off to England, where he enters St Paul's School in London in 1884 and King's College, Cambridge in 1890. Sri Aurobindo is a brilliant student and passes the I.C.S., but "fails" to appear for the riding test and is disqualified. After 13 years in England Sri Aurobindo returned to India on February 6, 1893 at the age of 20. He joined the Baroda State Service from 1897 to early 1906 and taught French and English at the Baroda college, before eventually becoming its Principal.

It was at that time that he started writing a series of articles "New Lamps for Old" in the Indu Prakash, a Marathi-English daily from Bombay. Sri Aurobindo realised quickly that passive resistance, constitutional agitation "a la Congress", was not the right path to achieve an independent India. In the true spirit of a yogi, he re-enacted the Baghavad Gita's great message: that violence is sometimes necessary, if it flows from Dharma -and Dharma then was the liberation of India. Thus he began contacting revolutionary groups in Maharashtra and Bengal and tried to co-ordinate their action. At Sri Aurobindo's initiative, P. Mitter, Surendranath Tagore and Sister Nivedita formed the first Secret Council for revolutionary activities in Bengal. But action was accompanied by inner vision: "While others look upon their country as an inert piece of matter, forests, hills and rivers, I look upon my country as the Mother. What would a son do if a demon sat on her mother's breast and started sucking her blood? I know I have the strength to deliver this fallen race. It is not physical strength - I am not going to fight with sword or gun, but with the strength of knowledge". In 1905, the terrible Lord Curzon partitioned Bengal. This divide-and-rule move was meant to break the back of Bengali political agitation and use the East Bengal Muslim community to drive a wedge between Hindus and Muslims, a policy that was to culminate in India's partition in 1947. Bengal responded to its partition with massive and unanimous protests in which many personalities took part, such as Rabindranath Tagore, Surendranath Banerjee, Bepin Chandra Pal. The ideal of Swadeshi, which called for the boycott of British goods, spread widely.

B.C. Pal then launched the famous English daily, Bande Mataram; Sri Aurobindo joined it and soon became its editor. Day after day, he jotted down his vision and tried to instil fire and courage in the nation through the pages of Bande Mataram: "Nationalism is not a mere political programme; Nationalism is a religion that has come from God; Nationalism is a creed which you shall have to live.. If you are going to be a Nationalist, if you are going to assent to this religion of Nationalism, you must do it in the religious spirit. You must remember that you are the instruments of God... Then there will be a blessing on our work and this great nation will rise again and become once more what it was in the days of spiritual greatness". But Sri Aurobindo had to fight against the Congress Moderates, who, it must be remembered came out openly for complete independence only in 1929, of whom he said: "There is a certain section of India which regards Nationalism as madness and they say Nationalism will ruin the country.. They are men who live in the pure intellect and they look at things purely from the intellectual point of view".

Sri Aurobindo was very clear in what was demanded of a leader of India: "What India needs at the moment is the aggressive virtues, the spirit of soaring idealism, bold creation, fearless resistance, courageous attack". But if the

Swaraj

moderates dismissed Sri Aurobindo as a "mystic", Lord Minto, then Viceroy of India, made no such mistake, calling him, "the most dangerous man we have to deal with at present". Thus Sri Aurobindo was arrested on May 2nd 1908, following a failed assassination attempt on a British judge by a nationalist belonging to his brother's secret society. Sri Aurobindo spent a year in jail, which proved to be the turning point of his life as he went through the whole gamut of spiritual realisations. When he came out, the nationalist movement had nearly collapsed and he set about giving it a fresh impetus, launching a new English weekly, the Karmayogin, as well as a Bengali weekly, Dharma. This following is an extract from his famous Uttarpara speech, where he speaks of his spiritual experiences in jail: "When it is said that India shall rise, it is the Santana Dharma that shall rise. When it is said that India shall be great, it is the Santana Dharma that shall be great... But what is the Hindu religion? It is the Hindu religion only, because the Hindu nation has kept it, because in this peninsula it grew up in the seclusion of the sea and the Himalayas, because in this sacred and ancient land it was given as a charge to the Aryan race to preserve through the ages. That which we call the Hindu religion is really the eternal religion, because it is the universal religion which embraces all others. If a religion is not universal, it cannot be eternal.... Santana Dharma IS nationalism"...

In mid-February 1910, news reached that the British had again decided to arrest Sri Aurobindo and close down the offices of the Karmayogin. By that time Sri Aurobindo had the vision that India was free, for the external events are always preceded by an occult happening, sometimes long before they become "fait accompli". Sri Aurobindo then received an "adesh", an inspiration that he must go to Pondichery, then under French rule. He settled there, with a few disciples, the number of whom slowly swelled, until it became known as the Sri Aurobindo Ashram. He wrote all his masterpieces and devoted the remainder of his life to bringing down what he called the "supramental manifestation on the earth". The great Sage passed away on 5 December 1950.

Hinduism, true Hinduism, was for Sri Aurobindo the basis for India's past greatness, it was also the essence of nationalism, the MEANS of liberating India and ultimately the foundation of the future India. Unfortunately, the leaders of the Indian National Congress did not have the same vision. Of these leaders, history has mostly remembered two, the most famous of all: Jawaharlal Nehru and Mahatma Gandhi.

Jawahrlal Nehru

Today Nehru's legacy is still holding India in its iron grip: the centralised, autocratic and inefficient Government, where everything is decided from Delhi, even matters which should be left to the states; the octopus-like bureaucracy, which no Government can get rid of: we have seen how the BJP and Prime Minister Vajpayee himself became the prisoners of that bureaucracy; the widespread corruption, a direct result of the state's interference in everything, which created these white elephants, the national enterprises, such as the State Bank of India, or Air India; the obsolete laws, which nobody dares to get rid of; the generations of Marxist-oriented intellectuals, who have made money and fame out of bashing Hindus; the fear of China, who is still able to work against India (giving its nuclear know-how and missiles to Pakistan, for instance) while pretending to be friendly. The list is long and utterly depressing. When will India be able to free itself of Nehru, the "father" of the nation?

Yet a few historians have seen through him. Nehru, writes Danielou, "was the perfect replica of a certain type of Englishman. He often used the expression 'continental people', with an amused and sarcastic manner, to designate French or Italians. He despised non-anglicised Indians and had a very superficial and partial knowledge of India. His ideal was the

Swaraj

romantic socialism of 19th century Britain. But this type of socialism was totally unfit for India, where there was no class struggle and where the conditions were totally different from 19th century Europe." (Histoire de l'Inde p. 349). It should be added that Nehru was not a fiery leader, maybe because of his innate "gentlemanship", and often succumbed not only to Gandhi's views, with which he sometimes disagreed, not only to the blackmailing of Jinnah and the hard line Indian Muslim minority, but also to the British, particularly Lord Mountbatten, whom history has portrayed as the benevolent last Viceroy of India, but who actually was most instrumental in the partition of India, whatever "Freedom at Midnight," a very romanticised book, says. (Remember Churchill's comment on learning about Partition: "At least we had the last word".) It may be added that the British had a habit of leaving a total mess when they had to surrender a colony, witness Palestine, or today's Ireland.

Mahatma Gandhi

Mahatma Gandhi was indeed a great soul, an extraordinary human being, a man with a tremendous appeal to the people. But, unfortunately, he was a misfit in India. Karma or fate, or God, or whatever you want to call it, made a mistake when they sent him down to the land of Bharat. For at heart, Gandhi was a European, his ideals were a blend of Christianity raised to an exalted moral standard and a dose of liberalism "à la Tolstoy". The patterns and goals he put forward for India, not only came to naught, but sometimes did great harm to a country which, unquestionably, he loved immensely. Furthermore, even after his death, Gandhism, although it does not really have any relevance to modern India, is still used shamelessly by all politicians and intellectuals, to smoke-screen their ineffectiveness and to perpetuate their power. To understand Gandhi properly, one has to put in perspective his aims, his goals, and the results today.

One has to start at the beginning. There is no doubt that after his bitter experiences with racism in South Africa, he took to heart the plight of fellow Indians there. But what did he achieve for them? Second class citizenship! Worse, he dissociated them from their black Africans brothers, who share the same colour and are the majority. And today, the Indians in South Africa are in a difficult position, sandwiched between the Whites who prefer them to the Blacks but do not accept them fully as their own, and the Blacks who often despise them for their superior attitudes. Ultimately, they sided with the moderate Whites led by De Klerk and this was a mistake, as Mandela was elected and the Blacks wrested total power in South Africa - and once more we might have an exodus of Indians from a place where they have lived and which they have loved for generations.

The Mahatma did a lot for India. But the question again is: what remains today in India of Gandhi's heritage? Spinning was a joke. "He made Charkha a religious article of faith and excluded all people from Congress membership who would not spin. How many, even among his own followers, believe in the gospel of Charkha? Such a tremendous waste of energy, just for the sake of a few annas is most unreasonable", wrote Sri Aurobindo in 1938 (India's Reb 207). Does any Congress leader today still weave cotton? And has Gandhi's khadi policy of village handicrafts for India survived him? Nehru was the first to embark upon a massive "Soviet type" heavy industrialisation, resolutely turning his back on Gandhi's policy, although handicrafts in India do have their place.

Then, nowhere does Gandhi's great Christian morality find more expression than in his attitude towards sex. All his life he felt guilty about having made love to his wife while his father was dying. But guiltiness is truly a Western prerogative. In India sex has (was at least) always been put in its proper place, neither suppressed, as in Victorian times, nor brought to its extreme perversion, like in the West today.

Swaraj

Gandhi's attitude towards sex was to remain ambivalent all his life, sleeping with his beautiful nieces "to test his brahmacharya", while advocating abstinence for India's population control. But why impose on others what he practised for himself? Again, this is a very Christian attitude: John Paul II, fifty years later, enjoins all Christians to do the same. But did Gandhi think for a minute how millions of Indian women would be able to persuade their husbands to abstain from sex when they are fertile? And who will suffer abortions, pregnancy and other ignominies? And again, India has totally turned its back on Gandhi's policy: today its birth control programme must be the most elaborate in the world - and does not even utilise force (except for a short period during the Emergency), as the Chinese have done.

For all the world, Gandhi is synonymous with non-violence. But once more, a very Christian notion. Gandhi loved the Mahabharata. But did he understand that sometimes non-violence does more harm than violence itself? That violence sometimes is "Dharma", if it is done for defending one's country, or oneself, or one's mother, or sisters? Take the Cripps proposals for instance. In 1942, the Japanese were at the doors of India. England was weakened, vulnerable and desperately needed support. Churchill sent Sir Stafford Cripps to India to propose that if India participated in the war effort, Great Britain would grant her Dominion status (as in Australia or Canada) at the end of the war. Sri Aurobindo sent a personal letter to the Congress, urging it to accept. Nehru wavered, but ultimately, Gandhi in the name of non-violence put his foot down and the Cripps proposal was rejected. Had it been accepted, history might have been changed, Partition and its terrible bloodshed would have been avoided.

Gandhi also never seemed to have realised the great danger that Nazism represented for humanity. A great Asuric wave had risen in Europe and threatened to engulf the world and it had to be fought - with violence. Calling Hitler "my beloved brother", a man who murdered 6 million Jews in cold-blood just to prove the purity of his own race, is more than just innocence, it borders on criminal credulity. And did not Gandhi also advise the Jews to let themselves be butchered?

Ultimately, it must be said that whatever his saintliness, his extreme and somehow rigid asceticism, Gandhi did enormous harm to India and this harm has two names: Muslims and Untouchables.

The British must have rubbed their hands in glee: here was a man who was perfecting their policy of divide-and-rule, for ultimately nobody more than Gandhi contributed to the partition of India, by his obsession to always give in to the Muslims, by his obstinate refusal to see that the Muslims always started the rioting - Hindus only retaliated; by his indulgence of Jinnah, going as far as proposing to make him the Prime Minister of India. Sri Aurobindo was very clear about Hindu-Muslim unity: "I am sorry they are making a fetish of Hindu-Muslim unity. It is no use ignoring facts; some day the Hindus may have to fight the Muslims and they must prepare for it. Hindu-Muslim unity should not mean the subjection of the Hindus. Every time the mildness of the Hindu has given way. The best solution would be to allow the Hindus to organise themselves and the Hindu-Muslim unity would take care of itself, it would automatically solve the problem. Otherwise we are lulled into a false sense of satisfaction that we have solved a difficult problem, when in fact we have only shelved it." (India's Rebirth, p. 159).

Gandhi's love of the Harijans, as he called them, was certainly very touching and sprang from the highest motivations, but it had also as its base a Christian notion that would have found a truer meaning in Europe, where there are no castes, only classes. Glorifying the scavenger as a man of God makes good poetry, but little social meaning. In the words of Sri Aurobindo: "the idea that it needs a special "punya" to be born a Bhangi is, of course one of these forceful exaggerations which are common to the Mahatma and impress greatly the mind of his hearers. The idea behind it is that his function is an indispensable service to society, quite as much as the Brahmin's, but that being disagreeable, it would need a special moral heroism to choose it voluntarily and he thinks as if the soul freely chose it as such a heroic service to the society and as reward of righteous acts - but that is hardly likely. In any case, it is not true that the Bhangi life is superior to the Brahmin life and the reward of special righteousness, no more that it is true that a man is superior because he is born a Brahmin. A spiritual man of pariah birth is superior in the divine values to an unspiritual and worldly-minded Brahmin. Birth counts but the basic value is in the soul behind the man and the degree to which it manifests itself in nature". (India's Rebirth, p.201).

Once more Gandhi took the European element in the decrying of the caste system, forgetting the divine element behind. And unfortunately he sowed the seeds of future disorders and of a caste war in India, of which we see the effects only today.

Non-violence, you say? But Gandhi did the greatest violence to his body, in true Christian fashion, punishing it, to blackmail others into doing his will, even if he thought it was for the greater good. And ultimately, it may be asked, what remains of Gandhi's non-violence to day? India has fought three wars with Pakistan, had to combat the Chinese, has the second biggest army in the world and has to fight counter-insurgency movements in Punjab, Assam and Kashmir. Gandhi must have died a broken man indeed. He saw India partitioned, Hindus and Muslims fighting each other and his ideals of Charhka, non-violence and Brahmacharya being flouted by the very men he brought-up as his disciples.

However, his heritage is not dead, for it survives where it should have been in the first instance: in the West. His ideals have inspired countless great figures, from Martin Luther King, to Albert Einstein, to Nelson Mandela, the Dalaï-Lama or Attenborough and continues to inspire many others. Gandhi's birth in India was an accident, for here there is nothing left of him, except millions of statues and streets and saintly mouthings by politicians, who don't apply the least bit of what Gandhi had taught so ardently.

History will judge. But with Nehru on one side and his westernised concept of India and Gandhi on the other, who tried to impose upon India a non-violence which was not hers, India was destined to be partitioned. Thus when the time came, India was bled into two, in three even, and Muslims took their pound of flesh while leaving. India never recovered from that trauma and today she is still suffering from its consequences. Yet has anybody really understood the lessons of history ?

P.S. The history of India's independence movement would be incomplete without mentioning the West's contribution. Perhaps the redeeming factor for the Britisher's utter insensitiveness, lies in Sister Nivedita's recognising India's greatness and consecrating her life and work not only to India but to its independence. The Theosophical Society started in 1875 by Mrs Blavatsky, a Russian and an American, Colonel Olcott, and brought to glory by Annie Besant, has also done a great deal to further abroad Hinduism's cause. Its philosophy is founded upon the recognition of Hinduism as one of the highest forms of revelation, as Mrs Besant wrote: "The action to pursue is to revitalise ancient India to bring back a renewal of patriotism, the beginning of the reconstruction of the nation". Unfortunately, the Theosophical Society often became bogged down in concentrating on the "magical mystical Orient".

Chapter 9

15ᵀᴴ August 1947

The first leaders of pre-independent India took some disastrous decisions, and the worst of them was to allow the division of their own country on religious lines. And today, the consequences of this partition are still felt : Kashmir is the most visible of them; but you also have Ayodhya, Kargil, the nuclear bomb, the Bombay or Coimbatore blasts, Godhra and, above all, the self-negation of a nation which is not whole, which has lost some of its most precious limbs in 1947. Yes, it is true, the British used to the hilt the existing divide between Hindus and Muslims; yes, the Congress was weak : it accepted what was forced down its throat by Jinnah and Mountbatten, even though many of its leaders, and a few moderate Muslims, disagreed with the principle of partition; it was also Gandhi's policy of non-violence and gratifying the fanatical Muslim minority, in the hope that it would see the light, which did tremendous harm to India and encouraged Jinnah to harden his demands. But ultimately, one has to go back to the roots, to the beginning of it all, in order to understand Partition. One has to travel back in history to get a clear overall picture. This is why memory is essential, this is why holocausts should never be forgotten.

For Jinnah was only the vehicle, the instrument, the avatar, the latest reincarnation of the medieval Muslims coming down to rape and loot and plunder the land of Bharat. He was the true son of Mahmud Ghaznavi, of Muhammed Ghasi, of Aurangzeb. He took up again the work left unfinished by the last Mughal two centuries earlier: 'Dar-ul-Islam', the House of Islam. The Hindu-Muslim question is an old one - but is it really a Hindu-Muslim question, or just plainly a Muslim obsession, their hatred of the Hindu pagans, their contempt for this polytheist religion? This obsession, this hate, is as old as the first invasion of India by the Arabs in 650. After independence, nothing has changed: the sword of Allah is still as much ready to strike the Kafirs, the idolaters of many gods. The Muslims invaded this country, conquered it, looted it, razed its temples, humiliated its Hindu leaders, killed its Brahmins, converted its weaker sections. True, it was all done in the name of Allah and many of its chiefs were sincere in thinking they were doing their duty by hunting down the Infidel. So how could they accept on 15th August 1947 to share power on an equal basis with those who were their subjects for thirteen centuries? "Either the sole power for ourselves, and our rule over the Hindus as it is our sovereign right, we the adorers of the one and only true God - or we quit India and establish our own nation, a Muslim nation, of the true faith, where we will live amongst ourselves".

Thus there is no place for idolaters in this country, this great nation of Pakistan; they can at best be 'tolerated' as second-class citizens. Hence the near total exodus of Hindus from Pakistan, whereas more than half the Muslim population in India chose to stay, knowing full well that they would get the freedom to be and to practice their own religion. In passing, the Muslims took their pound of flesh from the Hindus - once more - by indulging in terrible massacres, which were followed by retaliations from Sikhs and hard core Hindus, the ultimate horror. Partition triggered one of the most terrible exodus in the history of humanity. And this exodus has not ended: they still come by hundreds of thousand every year from Bangladesh, fleeing poverty, flooding India with problems, when the country has already so many of her own.

For French historian Alain Danielou, the division of India

was on the human level as well as on the political one, a great mistake : "It added to the Middle East an unstable state, Pakistan, and burdened India which already had serious problems". And he adds: "India whose ancient borders stretched until Afghanistan, lost with the country of seven rivers (the Indus Valley), the historical centre of her civilisation. At a time when the Muslim invaders seemed to have lost some of their extremism and were ready to assimilate themselves to other populations of India, the European conquerors, before returning home, surrendered once more the cradle of Hindu civilisation to Muslim fanaticism." (Histoire de l'Inde, p.355).

Pakistanis will argue that the valley of Kashmir, which has a Muslim majority, should have gone to Pakistan – and in the mad logic of partition they are not totally wrong. It is because Nehru and Gandhi accepted this logic, which was tremendously stupid, that India is suffering so much today. Of course, we cannot go back, history has been made : Pakistan has become an independent country and it is a "fait accompli". But if you go to Pakistan today, you will notice that its Punjabis look exactly the same as Indian Punjabis : they have the same mannerisms, eat the same food, dress similarly, speak the same language. Everything unites them, except religion. And this is what Sri Aurobindo kept saying in 1947 : "India is free, but she has not achieved unity, only a fissured and broken freedom...The whole communal division into Hindu and Muslim seems to have hardened into the figure of a permanent political division of the country. It is to be hoped that the Congress and the Nation will not accept the settled fact as for ever settled, or as anything more than a temporary expedient. For if it lasts, India may be seriously weakened, even crippled; civil strife may remain always possible, possible even a new invasion and foreign conquest. The partition of the country must go...For without it the destiny of India might be seriously impaired and frustrated. That must not be." (Message of Sri Aurobindo on the 15th of August 1947). It is only when the subcontinent will be whole again and the scars on both sides have been healed, that a Greater India will regain some of the self-pride gone with Partition.

All right, Nehru got his 'tryst with destiny', although a truncated tryst. India was free and everything was anew, the sky was the limit and a new glory was awaiting the land of Bharat. But what did Nehru and the Congress proceed to do with this new India? Writes Danielou: "The Hindus who had mostly supported the Congress in its fight for independence, had thought that the modernist ideology of an Anglo-Saxon inspiration of its leaders was only a political weapon destined to justify independence in the eyes of Westerners. They thought that once independence was acquired, the Congress would revise its policies and would re-establish proper respect towards Sanskrit culture, Hindu religious and social institutions, which form the basis of Indian civilisation. But nothing doing, the minority formed by the Congress leaders was too anglicised, to reconsider the value of what they had learnt. Few things changed in Indian administration, only the colour of the skin of the new rulers, who were most of the time lower ranks officials of the old regime". (Histoire de l'Inde, p. 348). And indeed, on top of the Partition tragedy, there is the other calamity of modern India: namely that under Nehru's leadership, it chose to turn its back on most of its ancient institutions, social and political, and adapted blindly and completely the British system, constitutional, social, political, judicial, and bureaucratic. For not only the greatness that WAS India was ignored, but, unconsciously it is hoped, it made sure that there would never be a greatness that IS India.

Democracy was then the new name of the game for India. But Sri Aurobindo had very clear ideas on "western democracy: "I believe in something which might be called social democracy, but not in any of the forms now current, and I am not altogether in love with the European kind, however great it may be an improvement upon the past. I hold that India, having a spirit of her own and a governing temperament proper to her own civilisation, should in politics as in everything else, strike out her original path and not stumble in the wake of Europe. But this is precisely what she will be obliged to do if she has to start on the road in her present chaotic and unprepared condition of mind". This was written, mind you, on January 5 1920 (India's Reb 143) and it was exactly what happened. Sri Aurobindo also felt: "The old Indian system grew out of life, it had room for everything and every interest. There was monarchy, aristocracy, democracy; every interest was represented in the government. While in Europe the Western system grew out of the mind: they are led by reason and want to make everything cut and dried without any chance for freedom or variation. India is now trying to imitate the West. Parliamentary government is not suited to India..."

Socialism certainly has its values, as Sri Aurobindo observed in 1914. "The communistic principle of society is intrinsically as superior to the individualistic as is brotherhood to jealousy and mutual slaughter; but all the practical schemes of socialism invented in Europe are a yoke, a tyranny and a prison."(India's Reb 99). "At India's independence, Nehru opted for what Danielou calls "romantic socialism". Was socialism best suited for India? It was maybe a matter for the best in the worst, to forestall a complete take-over by communism, which would have, as in China, entirely killed the soul of India and damaged for ever its Dharma. But if Nehru and the Congress leaders had not been so Anglicised and had known a little more of the exalted past of their country, they would have opted for a more Indianised system of socialism, such as the ancient panchayat system (which Rajiv Gandhi would attempt to revive later). Their socialism, although it was full of great and noble intentions, created great evils in India. Writes Danielou: "But this socialism was empty of meaning, for there existed no class struggle in India, nor social conditions similar to those in Europe. The controls established by a an incapable and corrupted bureaucracy, the ruin of private property, the incredible taxes slapped on capital, the confiscations, the dictatorial exchange controls, and the heavy custom duties, plunged India in a terrible misery. The lands of the zamindars were distributed to the poor peasants without any institution of agricultural financing, and farmers depending 100% on the loan shark were completely ruined and agricultural production went into a slump. The prohibition to export profits as well as the excessive taxes, forced all capitalist to flee the country." (Histoire de l'Inde p. 349).

One of the worst legacies of Nehru and the Congress is political. Like the British, Nehru centralised all the power at the Centre, the states were formed in an arbitrary manner and very little political autonomy was left to them. This created a land of babus and bred corruption. In turn, it triggered in certain states such as Tamil Nadu, whose culture has been preserved much more than in North Indian states, (maybe because it was more sheltered from Muslim incursions by the Deccan plateau), a resentment against the Centre, who was trying to impose Hindi on them, for instance, and fostered a seed of separatism. And why should the Centre try to impose Hindi on all Southern states? Hindi is a language which is spoken only by a few Northern states. And why, for that matter, should the Centre impose anything on the States, except in vital matters such as Security and External Affairs?

Nehru also initiated the entire bureaucratisation of India, which was a terrible mistake, if only because it was a system established by the British who wanted to centralise and control everything from the top. It was all right when the English were there, they were the masters, they made their riches out of plundering the country and had no need to be corrupt. But how do you give so much power to an insensitive babu, who earns only a few thousand rupees a month? Hence corruption and bureaucracy flourished together in India under Nehru.

The Soviet-type industrialisation, such as massive state industries, big steel mills, and mega dams, have already proved a failure in the West; yet Nehru and his successors all went for it. India became a state owned country which produced sub-standard quality goods. The only merit it had was to shelter her from a take-over by multinationals and allow her to develop her own products, however deficient.

Indians are so proud of their judicial system; but isn't it a carbon copy of the British one, with, as a consequence, a flurry of problems, whether it is the political interference in the naming of judges, the incredible backlog of pending cases, or the overcrowding of jails? Again, the Indian judiciary relies for its judgements on western values, on European jurisprudence, which are totally unfit for India. Once more, it is proud of its "secular" values and often comes down heavily on the fanatical bigots, meaning the Hindus. In education, Nehru carried on with the British policy of imposing a westernised English system: more and more the universities and schools of India, many of them run by Christians missions, produced a generation of English speaking diploma holders, who did not belong any more to Hindu society, but only to a fake bureaucratic society with westernised manners.

Finally, Hindu-bashing became a popular pastime under Nehru's rule. Jawaharlal had a great sympathy for communism like many men of his generation and indeed of the generations thereafter till the early 1970's. We have all been duped by communism, whose ideal is so appealing in this world of inequalities, but whose practise was taken over by Asuric forces, whether in Stalin's Russia, or in Maoist China. Nehru encouraged Marxist think-tanks, such as the famous JNU in Delhi, which in turn bred a lot of distinguished "Hindu-hating scholars" like Romila Thapar, who is an adept at negating Muslim atrocities and running to the ground the greatness of Hinduism and its institutions. Even today, most of the intellectuals, journalists and many of India's elite have been influenced by that school of thinking and regularly ape its theories. The sympathy of India's English media goes more towards Christians and Muslims, whatever excesses they commit, than to the majority Hindus, thanks to whom Christianity and Islam thrive in India. We have seen that bias time and again, whether after Graham Staines murder, or during the burning of the kar sevaks in the Sabamarti Express in Gujurat. This too is leftover from Nehruvianism.

But ultimately, whatever his faults, Nehru was part of India's soul. He fought for her independence with all his heart; and when freedom came, he applied to India the ideals he knew best, however misconceived they might have been. He was lucky enough to be in office while India went through a relatively peaceful period of her post-independence history, except for the first war with Pakistan and the China invasion. And he must have felt gratified to see his beloved country through the first stages of her recovery from the yoke of colonialism.

One does not want to dwell too much on communism in India, such as the one practised in Bengal or Kerala, although in its defence it must be said that on the one hand it is an Indian brand of communism, as the influence of Hinduism was able to soften it. On the other, that the Bengalis are too great a race to be completely bowled over by a thoroughly materialistic ideology. Naxalism also had its meaning: when one sees the injustice going on in India, with the amazing gap between the incredibly rich with black money, marrying their daughters off for lakhs of rupees in the five star hotels of Delhi - and the very poor, who can barely eat one meal a day, one feels like taking a gun and doing one's own justice. But once again this is not the way for India, for she has another wisdom waiting to be used again to solve all her problems without violence. What is the future of communism in India? Like the rest, it may be absorbed back in her psyche, transformed and adapted to her psychology, for even communism can find its place, as long as it recognises the central Dharma of India. Or maybe will it disappear altogether from the land of Bharat.

Chapter 10

20th century India : A Self-denial

Why is it that Indians, particularly its elite - the intelligentsia, the journalists, the writers, the top bureaucrats, the diplomats - hold an image of themselves which is often negative, and have a tendency to run down their own country ?

The self-perception that Indians have of themselves, is frequently detrimental to their self-confidence. This is particularly striking amongst Indian journalists, who always seem to look at India through a western prism and constantly appear to worry how the foreign press views India, how the foreign countries - particularly the United States of America - perceive India, what the Human Right agencies say about India. What matters to them is not what India's sages, avatars, gurus, wise men and yogis might utter - who dress Indian, eat Indian, think Indian and even dream Indian - but what the western media, or Amnesty International will think about India. They are not interested at all by what the Bhagavad Gita, probably the world's most revelatory, most comprehensive, most relevant sacred book has to say, or how Sri Sri Ravi Shankar, India's 21st century avatar, could help. No, they would rather turn to Thoreau, Marx or Jean-Paul Sartre, people who have even lost relevance in the West, for a solution to their immense problems.

Thus, when one reads certain Indian magazines, one has the impression that they could be written by foreign journalists, because not only do they tend to look at India in a very critical manner, but often, there is nothing genuinely Indian in their contents, no references to India's past greatness, no attempts to put things in perspective through the prism of India's ancient wisdom. Therefore, most of the time, their editorial contents endeavour to explain the present events affecting India, such as Ayodhya, or the problem of Kashmir, or the Christian missionaries' attempts at conversion of tribal Hindus, by taking a very small portion of the subcontinent's history - usually the most recent one - without trying to put these events in a broader focus, or attempting to revert back to India's long and ancient history. One could say - although things have been changing in the late nineties - that there is hardly any self-pride amongst India's intellectual elite, because they are usually too busy running down their own country. It is done in a very brilliant manner, it is true, - because Indian journalists, writers, artists, high bureaucrats, are often intelligent, witty and talented people - but always with that western slant, as if India was afflicted by a permanent inferiority complex. One then has to try to analyse the underlying reasons of this negative self-perception that India has of herself, probe the unconscious impulses which give many Indians - Hindus, we should say, as the majority of India's intelligentsia are born Hindus - the habit of always depreciating their own culture and traditions. And certainly, Nehru, his daughter Indira, Rajiv and the subsequent Congress leaders must be held partly responsible for this lack of confidence.

The Humiliation of 1962

The so-called Kargil war of Kashmir in June 1999 has triggered two very positive phenomenons for India. For the first time in a long stretch, it gave the country a bit of nationalism, it made many Indians proud of the heroism and selflessness of their soldiers. Whatever jingoism, or chauvinism there also was, one could feel, from Tamil Nadu to Punjab, that for a time there grew a feeling of togetherness in the nation, the knowledge of one's soldiers fighting it out there, in the harshest and most dangerous conditions and defending Mother India's sacred land. And that was very positive, for unless a nation possesses a bit of nationalism, it cannot keep on growing. And the second very positive aspect is that it has revived in India a notion which has been extinct for a long time : that of the Kshatriya spirit. A nation needs warriors, it needs soldiers to defend itself and protect its women, children, and its borders from hostile and Asuric elements, which throughout history have negated the Good and the Holy. It is fine to be Gandhian and non-violent, but in the tough and rough world of today, one cannot be too naïve: you need a strong and well-equipped army to be able to defend one's dharma. But a well equipped army is not enough – we have seen how today the United States' army, the most modern and high-tech of the world, is only capable of fighting from a distance, either bombarding from the sky, as they did in Yugoslavia or Afghanistan, or shooting from boats off-shore, a coward's war, as its soldiers have lost the sense of kshatriya, of honour, of dying for one's country. In Kargil, India saw the selflessness of its soldiers, with all the officers in front, climbing in the cold under enemy fire and wrestling peaks in impossible conditions, with little more than blood and tears.

But not only do Indians lack self-confidence in their dealings with the West, but they seem to have a permanent fear of the Chinese. Is it because in 1962, the Chinese took advantage of India's naïveté, and attacked treacherously in the Himalayas, humiliating the Indian army and taking away 20,000 square kilometres of her territory, which they have not yet vacated ? India's first Prime Minister, Jawarlahal Nehru, had decided that India and China were the natural 'socialist' brothers of Asia. Shortly before China's attack, the Indian Army Chief of Staff had drafted a paper on the threats to India's security by China, along with recommendations for a clear defence policy. But when Nehru read the paper, he said:

"Rubbish. Total Rubbish. We don't need a defence plan. Our policy is non-violence. We foresee no military threats. Scrap the Army. The police are good enough to meet our security needs." We know the results of this very foolish assessment.

But the biggest mistake that Nehru made was to betray Tibet, a peaceful spiritualised nation. For Tibet had always been a natural buffer between the two giants of Asia - in fact, the Dalai Lama's repeated offer that Tibet becomes a denuclearised, demilitarised zone between India and China, makes total sense today and Indian leaders should have immediately adopted it. But unfortunately, if there is one thing which all political parties in India share, it is the policy of appeasing China in exchange for a non-interference of the Chinese in Kashmir. But what non-interference ? Not only did China give Pakistan the know-how to develop nuclear weapons, but it also provided missiles to deliver them! On top of that, according to the CIA, China has transferred one third of its nuclear arsenal to Nagchuka, 250 kms away from Lhasa, a region full of huge caves, which the Chinese have linked together by an intricate underground network and where they have installed nearly one hundred Intercontinental Ballistic Missiles, many of them pointed at Indian cities. The reason for this is that the Chinese, who are probably among the most intelligent people in the world, have always understood that India is their number one potential enemy in Asia – in military, nuclear and economic terms.

It should be clear that as long as India does not stand-up to its responsibility towards Tibet and continues to recognise China's unjust suzerainty of it, there will be no peace in Asia. Indian leaders are perfectly aware that the Chinese, in span of fifty years, have killed 1,2 million Tibetans, razed to the ground 6254 monasteries, destroyed 60% of religious, historical and cultural archives and that one Tibetan out of ten is still in jail. As we enter the Third Millennium, a quarter million Chinese troops are occupying Tibet and there are 7,5 million Chinese settlers for six million Tibetans - in fact, in many places such as the capital, Lhasa, Tibetans are outnumbered two to one. India has also to wake-up to the plain fact that China needs space and has hegemonic aspirations: it got Tibet, it got Hong Kong, it got part of Ladhak; now it wants Taiwan, Arunachal Pradesh, the Spratly Islands and what not! Fifty years ago, during the Korean war, Sri Aurobindo, had seen clearly the Chinese game: "the first move in the Chinese Communist plan of campaign is to dominate and take possession first of these northern parts and then of South East Asia as a preliminary to their manoeuvres with regard to the rest of the continent in passing Tibet as a gate opening to India".

India should overcome its awe of China and be ready to eventually face once more the Chinese army. The nuclear tests of India, which have been very criticised, because ideally you have to get rid of nuclear weapons if you want a safe world, should be seen in that light.

Indira Gandhi

Indira certainly had a better understanding of the deeper, rural India than her father. But her legacy is still very bleak: she institutionalised the way the Congress still functions today, with its totally centralised pyramid-like system, with one person at the top wielding absolute power – and paved the way for Sonia Gandhi's absolute one-woman rule and the sycophancy surrounding her. Punjab and the Sikh problem were however the undoing of Indira; it poisoned the last years of her reign and finally killed her in the most frightful manner.

Wonderful religion that of Sikkism: the only true attempt ever to synthesise Hinduism and Islam - and who knows what would have happened if it had succeeded. "The Sikh Khalsa," writes Sri Aurobindo, "was an astonishingly original and novel creation and its face was turned not to the past but to the future. Apart and singular in its theocratic head and democratic soul and structure, its profound spiritual being, its first attempt to combine the deepest elements of Islam and Vedanta, it was a premature drive towards an entrance into the third or spiritual stage of human society, but it could not create between the spirit and the external life the transmitting medium of a rich creative thought and culture. And thus hampered and deficient it began and ended with narrow local limits, achieved intensity but no power of expansion..." (Foundations of Indian Culture, p. 380).

Unfortunately, the Sikhs, because they had to defend themselves against the terrible persecutions by the Muslims, became a militant religion, adopting hawkish habits, which even in time of peace they kept. And they also retained some of the more negative side of Islam: intolerance, or feeling of persecution, thus cutting themselves from the mainstream spirit of Hindu tolerance and width - from which they anyway came, and where they might ultimately go back.

Today, but even more during Indira Gandhi's time, Sikhism is on the defensive, or rather displays an aggressive spirit of defence. Why? As Sri Aurobindo points out, Sikhism was a wonderful attempt at synthesising Islam and Hinduism, but because the conditions were not right, it faltered. And today, whatever the loveliness of Sikh rites, the incredible beauty of the Golden Temple and its wonderful atmosphere; Sikhism, like Zoroastrianism of the Parsi community, may be a stagnating religion - whereas Hinduism from which Sikhism sprang in greater part, is very much alive and remains the Dharma, the source of all religions in India. It may be this unconscious realisation by the Sikhs that their religion is being slowly absorbed back into Hinduism, which triggers their militancy and fundamentalism. And after all, what is fundamentalism, but going back to the fundamentals, the foundations? And Sikhism strove best when it was militant, when it fought the Muslims; thus unconsciously, the separatists of the late seventies went back to that crease, to that glorious epoch to regain their identity. That is all that separatism is, a desperate attempt to regain Sikh identity in the face of the all pervasive and subtle Hindu onslaught. The fact that the British had planted that seed of separatism and that later it was fuelled, financed and armed by Pakistan, certainly did not help. But can the British, or Pakistan, or even Indira Gandhi be credited with having FABRICATED Sikh separatism? Mrs Gandhi was also accused of having 'created' Bhindranwale and made thus responsible for the whole Punjab problem. This is going to extremes; she may have politically helped Bhrinderwala and thought of using him later to counterbalance her opponents in Punjab. That's bad enough; but Bhrindhrawale's fanaticism and violence was his own, he was just an embodiment of Sikh militancy and frustration; if he had not been there, another Bhrindhrawale would have sprung-up, with or without Mrs Gandhi's help.

Finally, Sikhs and many other Indians have not forgiven Mrs Gandhi for giving the order of storming the Golden Temple. History will judge. But think of it this way: would the French Government have tolerated that for months, Basque separatists, for instance, be holed up in the Notre Dame Cathedral in Paris, the holiest of all Christian shrines, with their weapons, issuing deaths warrants against politicians, and receiving journalists, as Bhrindhrawale did? Certainly not. These Basque militants would not have lasted three days in Notre Dame; the army would have been called - and although great care would have been taken that no harm be done to the wonderful 1000 year old church, it would have been a fight to the finish. Remember also what happened to the 350 militants who took over the Kaba in Mecca in 1989? Most of them were killed when the Saudi government sent its special forces against what is the most sacred place of worship in the world to all Muslims. And what about the men, women and children barricaded up in Waco, Texas, with only a few guns: the FBI went in with flame throwers and armoured cars, killing so many innocents; and nobody in the world found anything to say. It is a credit to Indira Gandhi and the inherent Indian tolerance, that Bhrindhrawale and his followers were allowed to hole-up for so long in the Golden Temple. No democratic government in Europe or any Arab state would have allowed such a situation to continue. It was sad that the Golden Temple was damaged and so many were killed during the assault; but as the Head of Government, Mrs Gandhi took the correct decision. It was not her fault that the Sikhs allowed their most sacred place to become the shelter of men armed with weapons and with death in their hearts.

It is shameful that many Sikhs rejoiced when she was murdered in such a terrible way by her own Sikh bodyguards, men she had trusted, even though she had been told earlier to have all Sikhs removed from her personal security. To kill a woman lying on the ground with bullets, is a curse to any race that condones it. And ultimately, whatever her faults, Indira Gandhi - as she had predicted a few days before her assassination- did give her blood and her life for the country she loved in her own way. The vengeance of Hindus, backed by Congress leaders, was equally shameful and the culprits should be punished, it is never too late.

Rajiv

Rajiv Gandhi was typical of a certain breed of westernised Indians, totally ignorant about their own country, yet full of goodwill. It must be said in his defence that he was never interested in power, content to be a pilot, hobby around and live a quiet life with Sonia and his two children. But fate and his mother's distrust for everybody but her own sons, decided otherwise. It must also be said that the man (and his wife and children) demonstrated poise and dignity at his mother's assassination - and what a horrible way to lose one's mother - which could fill one's heart with hatred and ideas of vengeance. Rajiv showed in his early years goodwill and a sincere aspiration to transform the Indian system. But there were two problems: one was that being totally cut off from the Hindu reality of his country, he applied his effort to misconceived ideas about what India should be. And two, like Don Quixote battling the windmills, he had to fight the Congress system, its corruption and bureaucracy. In the end he gave-up this unequal battle and had to fall back on advice from the old guard. His ill-advised judgement in the Shah Bano case or his pandering to Palestine, were certainly more in tune with the old Congress policy of flattering the Indian Muslim community, as in the pre-independence Kalhifat movement, than his own opinions, for everything in his upbringing was pro-Western and Israel certainly was no enemy of his. He must have also secretly agreed with the Supreme Court judgement in the Shah Bano case.

If his mother's downfall and ultimate death was due to the Sikh separatist problem, his undoing was Sri Lanka and the Tamil separatist factor there.

Sri Lanka

There seems to be little doubt that once upon a time, not so long ago, India and Sri Lanka were linked by a small strip of land, which can still be seen today from the air: Adam's Bridge. And this is how the first Tamils, those who settled in the North, came to Sri Lanka (are they the first inhabitants of Sri Lanka and not the Sinhalese? This is another question!). There is also no doubt - and the Sinhalese recognise it - that they are originally Indians, although some say that they came from Gujurat, others from Bengal. Thus it can be established beyond doubt that Sri Lanka and India are one ethnically, although they differ in religion (but the same can be said within India). And throughout the ages, in one form or the other, Ceylon was under the influence of India. That is why, when the British conquered it in the late 18th century, they chose to attach it to their Indian empire. But when they left in 1947, in their desire to see that India never dominates too heavily the subcontinent, they facilitated the creation of Pakistan and handed to Sri Lanka its freedom. And India and Sri Lanka seemed to part ways for ever, as Tamils and Sinhalese were left to war with each other, until Rajiv sent the IKPF in 1988.

One has to go back a long time to understand what decisive factors shaped the psyche of the island's two communities. And this decisive factor bears the names of two of the world's greatest religions: Buddhism and Hinduism. The first one, Buddhism, is a gentle, peaceful creed, that teaches non-violence and brotherhood, even to enemies. Unfortunately Ceylon, often called the "isle of beauty", has always been too tempting a prey for sea-faring invaders. And indeed, successive colonisers, from Arabs to Africans, from Portuguese to Dutch and finally, British, preyed on the tiny, defenceless island. In the name of Buddhism and because the Sinhalese are by nature a fun-loving, gentle people, not only did they hardly resist these invasions, but often, many of their women mingled freely with the foreign intruders. The result can clearly be seen today on the faces of many Sinhalese women folk, with their African-curled hair, Arabic features and fair skinned faces. As a result, the Sinhalese slowly lost their sense of identity, their feeling of being a collective being, to the point that when the British came, they collaborated wholehearted with them and had to be handed back their independence on a platter, for want of a real freedom movement. Today, democracy and western institutions are just a flimsy cloak that the Sinhalese wear. Lurking underneath the pleasant, sometimes servile attitude towards Westerners, is a sense of hopelessness and a terrible violence. And in reality, since independence, Sinhalese politicians must have been some of the least farsighted of the entire subcontinent: nothing is made in Sri Lanka, everything has to be imported and only tea, tourism and Western grants, help the country survive.

On the other hand, Hinduism with its strict caste hierarchy, which forbids much contact with outsiders, particularly sexual contact with foreigners, protected Sri Lankan Tamils from mingling with their invaders. Thus they preserved their identity, their racial purity and their culture. Sinhalese live an easier life in the South, which was always more fertile than the arid North. As a result, Tamils have often been better at studies and more hard working. This was quickly noticed by the British, who often gave Tamils preference for jobs and university grants, thus angering the Sinhalese, who after all were the majority community.

It is this deep-rooted resentment of the Sinhalese towards the Tamil community which is the cause of the present troubles. When the British left, the Sinhalese quickly moved in to correct what they saw as an imbalance: they set on depriving the Tamils of most of the rights they had acquired under the British and proceeded to establish a Sinhalese-dominated Ceylon. And every time a Sinhalese politician tried to give the Tamils their just share of power, he quickly had to backtrack under Sinhalese resentment. For years, the Tamils bore the brunt of Sinhalese persecution. But one day, too much became too much and Tamil armed groups started springing up to defend their people. To cut short a long story, the LTTE finally emerged as the most ruthless and sole militant organisation. For those who remember the Tamil Tigers in their early years: young, bright, soft spoken university students, there was no doubt that they had started with a genuine aspiration to secure their just rights. But violence breeds its own violence and today the Tigers have lost all sense of measure and restraint, eliminating ruthlessly all that they think stands in the way of their freedom.

Yet, in 1988, Rajiv stepped in to mediate between the

warring Sinhalese and Tamils. All kinds of insulting epithets have been thrown onto the Jeyawardene-Rajiv Gandhi peace plan and the IPKF's role in Sri Lanka, but these are unfair (as unfair as accusing Mrs Gandhi of creating the Sri Lankan imbroglio by arming and sheltering the Tamil separatist groups in Tamil Nadu's coastal area. Those who vent these accusations have no knowledge of Sri Lankan history: 1) the problem goes back to 2000 years of strife. 2) The Tamils were at that time genuinely persecuted and faced pogroms. Short of India intervening militarily, it made sense to arm the Tamils so that they could defend themselves. The Rajiv Gandhi peace plan was the best attempt that could be made in the circumstances, to solve the ethnic war and ensure the region's stability - and the IPKF did not come to conquer and colonise, but to help. The LTTE betrayed the hand that had fed it, because it wants total and unequivocal freedom and it saw India's move as thwarting it (that is the main reason for their murdering Rajiv Gandhi. If he had come back to power, as indeed he was sure to, he would have pressurised the Sinhalese to grant the Tamils a semi-autonomous region in the North-East). But that is another matter. India thus got bogged down in a guerrilla war it did not want to fight, with one hand tied behind the back to avoid killing civilians; and ultimately it had to leave because of pressure at home and Mr Premadasa's intense dislike of Indians.

Today, Tamils have actually come one step nearer to freedom. The partition of Sri Lanka may be considered a "fait accompli". It might take some time, but ultimately, some Sinhalese leader will have to come to the conclusion that Sri Lanka's economy cannot be bled any more by this senseless war. What happens if one day the island's one million Tamil tea planters, (whose forefathers were "imported" from India by the British, another parting gift from dear Britannia), who up to now have kept away from the conflict, join hands with their North-East brothers? It would be the end of Sri Lanka.

And how long can tourism, the island's other source of revenue, be promoted in the midst of strife? The LTTE have chosen for the moment to leave the tourists alone. But it would be enough that they kill a few, to scare away Sri Lanka's main source of revenue.

But even if the partition of Sri Lanka is granted by the Sinhalese, with the north-east portion for the Tamils, the island will remain a hotbed of uncertainty, a potential time bomb in South Asia.

And this raises the question of India's security. At the moment, the Norwegians seem to have brokered a truce between the Sinhalese and the Tamil Tigers. But time and again the Tigers have used these truces to rearm and regroup, as their ultimate goal seems to be partition. What should be New Delhi's reaction in case of a Sri Lankan partition? Can India remain unaffected by whatever is going to happen in Sri Lanka? There are 55 millions Indian Tamils in Tamil Nadu. It has been shown already that instability in Sri Lanka breeds instability in Tamil Nadu. Certainly, Mrs Jayalalitha's autocratic ways, her godlike worship by her party men and her paranoia for security, which is justified by the terrible assassination of her friend Rajiv, are a direct result of Sri Lanka's strife. This frightful cold-blooded murder of Rajiv Gandhi was a consequence of the Sri Lankan problem, which India cannot ignore.

And ultimately, it is hoped that history will remember Rajiv with indulgence and affection, even if he had little understanding of India's true reality and her spiritual genius had completely eluded him. He was a gentleman and one always courteous with everybody, including journalists. Like his mother, he also gave his life for India and his terrible death shocked millions of us that fateful night in Sriperambadur. Apart from his goodwill, he must be credited with having started the economic liberalisation of India, indispensable if this country wants to become a 21st century superpower. Has the long Nehru dynasty ended with him?

PS. * A word about Bofors is a must, as it ended Rajiv Gandhi's first and only tenure as Prime Minister. The Indian Press has made too much of the Bofors controversy and the whole thing is a hypocrite's scandal, as all political parties in the world use kickbacks on arms deals to finance their election campaigns. Rajiv must have been convinced by the old Congress guard to accept the Bofors kickbacks for the party through intermediaries - and lived to regret it, trapped as he was in his lies.

** The less we talk about his successor, V.P. Singh, the better. Here was a man of talent, certainly, but of an immense ambition under the guise of a Gandhian cloak. To achieve his lifetime ambition of becoming Prime Minister, he did not hesitate to betray his own leader, Rajiv Gandhi. It should be remembered too, that he withdrew Rajiv's special security, when he knew very well that the man was on the hit list of not only the Sikh militants but also of the Tamil separatists. His own conscience will be judge for that act.

V.P. Singh also did immense harm to India. His implementation of the Mandal Report, was only a move at assuring his re-election, even at the cost of splitting the country on caste lines. Who will ever be able to forget the images of V.P. Singh's police shooting on students? There was an Asuric force at work, of which V.P. Singh was only one of the instruments. With him would come Mulayam Singh, Laloo Prasad, and Kanshi Ram, who would also use the caste factor to divide India and achieve their political ambitions.

Chapter 11

The Bharatiya Janata Party Years

Western correspondents - and unfortunately also Indian journalists - keep labeling the BJP and organizations to which the BJP owes some of its ideologies - such as the RSS, or the VHP - as "Hindu nationalists", or "Hindu fundamentalists". But this is a totally false and misleading statement, as in the whole history of India, Hindus - who let us remember, are 850 millions today and constitute the overwhelming cultural and political majority of this country - have not only shown that they are extremely tolerant, but Hinduism is probably the only religion in the world which never tried to convert others or conquer other countries to propagate their own religion. This historical tolerance of Hinduism is never taken into account by foreign correspondents covering India and even, unfortunately, by Indian journalists.

On the other hand, Hindus suffered immensely at the hands of the two greatest "monotheists" religions of the world. And it is only in the last eighty years that some " nationalist" movements were born to try to preserve Hindu culture in the face of conversions by Christian missionaries and the rising influence of the Muslim League. These movements, whose descendants today are the RSS, the Shiv Sena or the VHP, may make preposterous statements - although that is debatable - but they have never killed anybody, never massacred anybody in the name of their God. Burning down a few makeshift churches, however reprehensible these acts are, does not make them nazis or even dangerous fundamentalists. Let's respect the proper use of words.

In 1984, the Bharatiya Janata Party bagged only two seats in the general elections, a total humiliation. Twelve years later, in 1996, it became the largest party in India with 186 MPs and came briefly to power, even though its government was unfairly toppled ten days later. After the disastrous Governments of Mr Gowda and LK Gujral, a well meaning but largely ineffective man, the BJP came back to power at the head of a 18 parties coalition in March 1998 and did fairly well, although its hands were tied down by demanding allies, particularly by Jayalitha, the unpredictable "diva" of Tamil Nadu. The Indian voter was grateful for the handling of the Kargil war by Prime Minister Atal Behari Vajpayee, when the Pakistanis traitorously took advantage of the Lahore peace process initiated by India in February 1999, to infiltrate Pakistani soldiers disguised as mujahidins on the Indian side of the Line of Control in Kashmir. The Indian soldiers performed very bravely in the face of tremendous odds and the international community appreciated India's restraint in not crossing over onto the Pakistani side of the LOC.

This is why, after Sonia Gandhi, with the help of Jayalitha, toppled the BJP Government once more, with the covert help of the President of India and the Election Commissioner, the Indian electorate returned to power the BJP and its allies with a thumping majority, although the BJP itself did not do as well as expected, specially in Uttar Pradesh. Regrettably, the BJP, in its desire to appear "secular", forsook many of the ideals which had made it dear and unique in the eyes of many of India's voters, thus taking the road charted by the Congress before them. It did not take advantage of the unprecedented popularity it enjoyed once upon a time, of a new feeling of "nationalism", to come-up with some hard

The Bharatiya Janata Party Years

decisions, so as to "Indianise" the nation that it may manifest again its true unique soul : give back the power to the villages in the form of Panchayat. Re-introduce Sanskrit as the national language. Rewrite Indian History, which had mostly been devised by White Masters. Revive ancient traditional systems such as pranayama, yoga, and incorporate them in the education system and everyday life. Change the constitution so that democracy may not be perverted as it is today. Privatise the numerous "white elephants", such as many of the Indian banks, SAIL, ITDC, etc. Unfortunately, there has already been, at the time when this book goes to press, a certain amount of "Congressisation" of the BJP in power and many of the Hindu groups, like the RSS, are disappointed with the BJP leaders, although some of the Ministers, such as Dr. Murli Manohar Joshi have tried to fulfill the prophecy of Sri Aurobindo : "India of the ages is not dead nor has She spoken Her last creative word. And that which She must seek now to awake, is not an anglicised oriental people, docile pupil of the West and doomed to repeat the cycle of the Occident's success and failure, but still the ancient immemorial Shakti recovering Her deepest self, lifting Her head higher towards the supreme source of light and strength and turning to discover the complete meaning and vaster form of Her Dharma".

Today, India is still viewed with suspicion by foreign Governments, although things are beginning to change, because this country is the leading exporter in the world of software programs and Indians abroad are making a mark for themselves. But let us remember how in the sixties, China was to the world a backward nation, the "Red Devil". Richard Nixon's visit there in 1971, changed everything: today, it is a must for industrialised nations to invest there, even if the returns are very poor and China is bound sooner or later to enter into grave political turmoil when the bloody hand of communism is withdrawn. India's eventual admission in the Security Council of the UN will signal to the world that India is the next superpower of this century, the "other" democratic giant of Asia and that it is time for the West to start doing business with India.

"Nostradamus and the BJP"

Here below are extracts of a spoof I wrote in 1999 for my Ferengi's column of the Indian Express. Was it prophetic? Only time will tell.

Michel de Nostre-Dame, better known as Nostradamus (1503-1566), was a famous French astrologer whose predictions - which included the assassination of John Fitzgerald Kennedy, or the premature death of the previous Pope - have proved infallibly accurate.

Last month, unpublished manuscripts of Nostrodamus have been discovered (and authentified) in an old trunk in the French city of Lyon. Curiously, there are two full pages, which deal at length with India, particularly with the Bharatiya Janata Party and the just concluded elections. We are giving here the first words in Latin, the language which he used, along with a rough translation in English.

"Politicus Bharatus Janatus Indicus veni grandus est vingtus unus centurus - Congressus oublium est ..."

The Bharatiya Janata Party will come to dominate India in the beginning of the 21st century, as the Congress will slowly sink into oblivion.

"Malheureusus, duo annum millenium trahisonus idealum est Congressus ressemblum, fautum adoptus est. Electionirium Blanca Madamus attaquum".

Unfortunately, to achieve power, the BJP may gradually forsake most of its idealism and it will not address the real burning changes which India needs to adopt so as to become again a Great Power".

The Bharatiya Janata Party Years

And Nostradamus goes on to enumerate these changes:

"Congressus independantum Blancum copium est; necessarus changum indianus cumum facus est"...

As the Congress had heavily borrowed from the White Man (British ?) at Independence, it will become necessary to "Indianise" the nation so that it may manifest again its true unique soul.

"Panchayatum villagum empruntus. Sanskritus introdum est. Historicum ecritum manus, daemonus est. Yogum, respirationnus introdum est."

Give back the power to the villages in the form of Panchayat. Reintroduce Sanskrit as the national language. Rewrite Indian History, which had mostly been devised by White Masters. Revive ancient traditional systems such as pranayama, yoga, and incorporate them in the education system and everyday life. Change the Constitution so that democracy may not be perverted as it will be

"Malheureusus, secularus montrarus Congressus devenium est, corptionus introdus cancerus est."

Unhappily again, goes on to say Nostradamus, the BJP in its eagerness to prove itself secular (secularus is originally a Latin word), will tend to become like the Congress: corruption, bureaucracy, the VIP plague, the madness of subsidies and the hunger for power, may eat its inner core as a cancer.

And this is Nostradamus' scoop - if we may say:

"Politicus Bharatus Janatus interminum dividus duum et novus politicus formus".

After some time, the Bharatiya Janata Party may split into two. Sincere idealists will form a parallel party which will have as its political platform many of the ideals which the BJP had forsaken.

"Indianus pretus reformus est, Grandus nationus manum".

India by that time will be ready for the Big Change and the new party will sweep the polls and implement these reforms.

"Sanskritus savantuus nationalum languus, decentralisum governmentus, aryanus theorum mortuum est, dharmum hinduus devenum. Christianum, Islamus influencum".

Scholars will sit down to modernize and simplify Sanskrit; government will be decentralised; India will strive to form a federation of SAARC countries; the theory of the Aryan invasion will be proved false and it will be shown that Indian civilisation is at least ten thousand years old and has influenced all great ancient civilisations and religions such as Christianity and even Islam.

And finally:

"Aurobindus Ghosus realisum est, Indianum Agus ancientus mortum non est."

And the prophecy of Sri Aurobindo will be fulfilled: "India of the ages is not dead nor has She spoken Her last creative word. And that which She must seek now to awake, is not an anglicised oriental people, docile pupil of the West and doomed to repeat the cycle of the Occident's success and failure, but still the ancient immemorial Shakti recovering Her deepest self, lifting Her head higher towards the supreme source of light and strength and turning to discover the complete meaning and vaster form of Her Dharma".

Sonia Gandhi and the Future of the Congress

When Sonia Gandhi took over the reins of the Congress beginning of 1998, it was thought that the party would revive

The Bharatiya Janata Party Years

its fortunes with her leadership. After all, was she not the inheritor of the Gandhi-Nehru dynasty ? But under her rule, the Congress had disastrous showings at the polls, particularly during the 1999 elections, where it only got 112 seats, a rout royal; the party did not do well either in the recent UP elections, coming in third place behind Mulayam's party and the BJP. Yet, no voices were raised after these debacles to ask for her resignation, nobody, except Pawar and Sangma dared to challenge her autocratic ways, her absolute control over huge funds and foundations, her aloofness, surrounded as she is by security, sycophants and secretaries. Why is that? Everything possible has been said to explain how Congressmen, big and small, important and humble, have been humiliating and are still debasing themselves in front of Sonia Gandhi. There is sycophancy, of course : it is an old Congress tradition, although it should be said that Indian sycophancy is a perverted offshoot of bhakti, the great Hindu tradition of worshipping "That" which seems to be above us, regardless of its value; there is obviously self interest - most of the Congress bigwigs, who are much more intelligent than they are given credit for, know that without Sonia (or Nehru / or Rajiv / or Indira), they stand to get very few votes; there is the dynasty rule angle - but again, dynasty is a very western word, which applies more to the American soap opera of the same name, than to India, where the concept of bhakti, coupled with the old maharaja tradition, have always ensured respects for "royal" families; there is the foreign angle, naturally: let us not forget that the Congress was founded by a Scot, A.O. Hume, and that for a long time it was manipulated by its British masters to ensure that India stayed with the Crown, with Sonia, another foreigner at its helm, Congress has come full circle; lastly, there is an element which has been overlooked: the shakti element, which is so strong and prevalent in India, that it allowed Indira Gandhi to govern with an iron hand this male-dominated country for nearly twenty years and that it has even survived in the neighboring Islamic states, such as Pakistan or Bangladesh, witness Benazir Bhutto or the two Bangla Begums. But the main cause for this fascination that Sonia Gandhi, whatever her merits (and she did put some order and dignity back in the Congress), exercises on Indians in general, whether they love or hate her, is the Great Myth of the Aryan Invasion of India, of which we have spoken earlier. It is because of this Aryan myth that dark-skinned Indians of humble origin dream of having a white skin; it is because of this myth that even the upper-class Indians think that everything Aryan - read White - is better than their own culture; it is because of this myth that Indians come by droves to witness in person the White Skin of Sonia Gandhi when she comes to their areas to address a rally, even if they might not vote for her.

What is the future of Congress in 21st century India then? If it wants to be a worthy opposition party to the BJP,or whoever is in power , it should get rid of its hankering for the dynasty rule, and find within its ranks young and dynamic leaders - and there are quite a few waiting in the wings (although sadly, two of their best youthful leaders, Rajesh Pilot and Scindia, died in accidents), more than the BJP even, where leaders are quite old generally. It should also look at the past in a frank and open manner and acknowledge the great blunders committed by the Congress since the beginning of the century: the pandering to the Muslim League by Gandhi, specially the horrifying Khalifat episode, the partition of India, for which Gandhi was also greatly responsible, the disastrous "socialist" policies of Nehru, his cowardly attitude towards China and Tibet, which led to the humiliation of the Indian army in 1962, the constant Hindu-baiting by the Nehruvian intelligentsia and Congressmen since 1926, and finally the catastrophic rules of Indira and Rajiv Gandhi, who, whatever their goodwill, had no inkling about India's great past and potential spiritual future. Only then will the Congress have a chance to redeem itself and find a meaningful place in History books.

Chapter 12

The Threats at the Hands of Indians Themselves

The worst enemies of Indians... are Indians... and very often they are Hindus! It is true that Hinduism has always been the target of India's external enemies: Muslim invaders, Christian missionaries, or English colonisers, but ultimately, if Hindus were united – let us remember that there are 1,1 billion of them today throughout the world, the third largest religion - nothing could happen to them.

Kashmir

Very few foreign (and Indian journalists) know that in Srinagar you can still find a small Hindu temple on the banks of the river Jhelum, lost amongst the hundred and one mosques of Srinagar. Its entrance is always heavily guarded by BSF forces and it is protected by sandbags on all sides, as it has been hit a few years ago by a rocket fired by Muslim militants. Inside, a handful of Kashmri Pandits are still trying to preserve this sacred place, where a natural lingam is said to have emerged 3000 years ago and where their forefathers have worshipped for twenty generations. There were once 30,000 Hindus in Srinagar, but today only a handful are left. At the beginning of the century, a million Hindus were found in the valley of Kashmir, 300,000 in 1947; today 98% of the Kashmiri Pandits have fled the Valley of Kashmir: their houses were burnt, their women raped, their sons killed. Why does nobody ever mention these facts?

Western journalists prefer to report on the Indian army's "atrocities" in Kashmir. Which reminds one of an incident in May 1998, during elections. The day before, the Government had all the separatist leaders put under house arrest, as a precautionary measure. But one of them, Yasim Malik, managed to slip away. His aides called the local stringers to warn them that he would surface on election day, near the Jamma Masjid. Thus, on 30th May, a caravan of about 35 cars, with eager, impatient, news-hungry journalists on board, blasted its way towards the mosque. And there, sure enough, at 10 a.m., Yasim Malik, looking more sickly than ever, appeared with about three to four hundred Kashmiris. The loudspeakers of the mosque started blaring out slogans and as the BBC team headed by a very senior and famous British reporter (who later became an MP) arrived, the Kashmiris began getting hysterical: the woman wailed, the men shouted and gesticulated. Journalists were in ecstasy: the BBC cameraman zoomed onto the crowd and the foreign photographers pushed each other to get a shot of Yasim Malik, who said something like: "this election will happen only over our dead bodies". Suddenly, the crowd, which so far had kept within the mosque's compound, poured out through the gates and started throwing stones at the BSF, which in turn had to lob tear gas and shot in the air. Immediately, as if by magic, everyone vanished. An Indian cameraman working for a foreign network, obviously getting very scared, screamed: "I have them on film shooting, I have them shooting; let's get out of here". And the 35 cars wound back full speed on their way to the hotels, the journalists to file their story, the photographers to print their photos and the cameramen to edit their story. Everybody was happy, because as one European photographer put it: "that was good, exciting stuff". The same night and the next day, BBC, CNN and other networks beamed world-wide stories of "widespread violence in Kashmir" and of "intimidation of voters" (which nobody actually saw on that day). The BBC footage, which cleverly zoomed tight all the

The Threats at the Hands of Indian Themselves

time on the gesticulating Kashmiris, made it appear as if a few thousand demonstrators were there, when actually they were only a couple of hundred; and great use was made of the police firing their guns in the air.

Ultimately, the truth must be said: we foreign journalists all come to Kashmir to get our pound of flesh. Our stories cannot be good and complete unless we can harp at human rights in Kashmir, speak of torture, rape, custody killings and generally berate the bad Indian army, because this is what our editors expect of us. Thus, most of us have already - at least subconsciously - set our mind to what we are going to say, even before setting foot in Kashmir. And the same can be said of most of the western diplomats who come to Kashmir on fact-finding missions for their government. Often, before they get down to write their reports, they have already decided what they are going to say - and even if they haven't, they ultimately will. The reason is simple: both journalists and diplomats depend on two sources for their reporting in Kashmir: one is the stringers of Indian newspapers, who happen to be mostly Kashmiris. Publicly and in their writings, they have to be careful about what they say; but privately, specially in the presence of western journalists, whom they expect to share their feelings, they usually vent their hatred of India. And the second source is the taxi drivers of Srinagar, who are controlled by a handful of operators, who book hotels, get airline tickets confirmed, arrange meetings with separatists leaders, even with militants, or bring foreigners to houses where Kashmiri women have been supposedly raped and generally shape the mind of their protégés. Needless to say - and that is only fair - they have only one goal: to show the great suffering of the Kashmiri people at the hands of the Indian imperialists. Recently the number two of a very important European Embassy based in Delhi was seen in the house of one of these operators; and although he was a little embarrassed, there was no doubt that his mind had already been made up on what he was going to report.

But the question is: are Indian journalists better? Well, sometimes they seem to want to outdo westerners in sensationalism, maybe to show that they are truly "secular". What about this Indian newspaperman, whom we shall call N., working for a famous Human Rights agency based in Delhi, which is sponsored by German money. Everyday during the elections in Srinagar, he would proudly show us his "home work", thinking it would please us: "BSF broke into a house of two Kashmiris, and beat father and son", before faxing it to his office in Delhi. Good work. But why do none of these so-called human rights organisations ever bother to meet those pandits who are courageously staying behind to guard one of the rare Hindu temples still standing in Kashmir? True the Kashmiri Muslims have genuine grievances: the Congress once rigged elections in their state, toppled their elected government, bought their leaders... But the story is the same everywhere in India. In fact, Kashmir is and has always been a privileged and pampered place. Indians are not allowed to buy land in Kashmir, but Kashmiris, who are very good businessmen, have had no qualms about investing in India and setting up flourishing businesses all over the country. The Indian Government keeps pouring crores of rupees in to Kashmir. But if these people really want their independence, shouldn't they be straightforward about it and stop using Indian money and utilising the Government of India's services to export their carpets? It is also true that the 36% participation in the elections does not seem quite realistic. But the situation in Kashmir has become very complex: you have the renegades who voted, the Kashmiri pandits who voted by mail; then there are also those Kashmiris who genuinely wanted to vote, and others who voted out of fear either of the army, or of the renegades. And after all, this high percentage of voters might be a sign that some of the people are getting fed-up with militancy.

While India should definitely work on its human rights record in Kashmir and elsewhere, it should also ignore the moralising discourses of the West, which stinks of hypocrisy. After all, if the British fought to keep the Falkland islands, thousands of miles away from Great Britain; if Spain battles the Basques separatists; if France refuses to let go of Corsica - an island at that - why should India feel guilty about retaining what has been hers for 5000 years? The militants have initiated a reign of violence, murder and rape and the Indian army had to fight back with the same weapons, albeit ruthlessly. Kashmiris have only themselves to blame for their misery: you do not fight a counterinsurgency movement with flowers and polite talk.

Indian Muslims: Babar Or Ram?

Indian Muslims are today at a crossroads. The destruction of the Buddhist statues in Afghanistan, then later, the terrorists attacks on America of September 2001, have shown to the world in general – and to the Muslims of India in particular – that Islam still considers as kafirs not only the Buddhists, Hindus and Jews of this world, but also the great "American Satan". Today, in Bangladesh, Afghanistan, or in Pakistan, Hindu statues and temples can still be razed and the Infidels eliminated. The Taliban and Al Qaida movement may have been partially wiped-out by the Americans, but they will be reborn somewhere else under a different name. Because for the fundamentalist Muslims and those who support them, covertly or overtly, nothing has changed since Mohamed broke the first 'idol' statues in the 7th century and the task has been left unfinished. The increasing suicide attacks on the Indian army by Islamic groups, still supported and financed by Pakistan, in spite of its commitment to do away with State sponsored terrorism, should also prove that the Islamic injunction of jihad is very much alive and in practice in much of the Islamic world, from Sudan to Libya, from Saudi Arabia to Pakistan.

The question that Indian Muslims should ask themselves

now is simple: "who are we"? Amongst the 120 million Muslims in India, only a tiny percentage descends from the Turks, Afghans, or Iranians who invaded India. The majority of them are converted Muslims. And converted how? By terror, coercion, force, bloodshed. The ancestors of today's Indian Muslims are probably those who suffered the most from the Arab and Muslim invasions. Those Hindus and Sikhs who chose not to convert, took refuge in their faith, fought together and kept their pride and honor. The first two generations of those who converted must have endured hell: for they certainly did not convert out of conviction, but because they had no choice: their daughters and wives were raped, sons taken into slavery, parents killed. It is sad today that their descendants have sometimes made theirs the intolerant cry of Islam.

It is true that many Indian Muslims were Hindu untouchables. Marxists would like us to believe that they converted because they thought that they would access the more egalitarian society of Islam. What rubbish! Does one think in that way in time of war, terror and tears? Do today's Hindu lower castes convert to Islam when there is no more violent coercion? More likely, the untouchables were the most vulnerable, the least apt to defend themselves; they had neither the faith of the Brahmins, nor the riches of the Vaishiyas, nor the military skill of the Kshatriyas. Do Indian Muslims understand that they were part of the richest, most advanced, most tolerant and generous civilization of ancient times. That their culture was so advanced that it had spread all over the world? Do they realise that more and more archeological and historical discoveries are pointing out that the genocide of Hindus by Muslim invaders is without parallel.

Islam cannot be wished away. As Sri Aurobindo said "Mahomed's mission was necessary, else we might have ended by thinking, in the exaggeration of our efforts at self-purification, that earth was meant only for the monk and the city created as a vestibule for the desert". Thus Indian Muslims

The Threats at the Hands of Indian Themselves

have to keep their faith and any attempt by Hindus to convert them back is not only futile but counterproductive. But the question to be asked to them is: "what kind of Islam do you want to practice? An Islam which looks westwards, towards a foreign city, the Mecca, swears by a Scripture, the Koran, which is not only not relevant to India, but which was meant for people living 1500 years ago, in a language which is not Indian? Or do they want to practice an Islam which is "Indianised", which accepts the reality of other Gods, as Hinduism and Buddhism accept that there have been other avatars than Ram or Buddha.

Do India's Muslims want to worship Babar, a man who destroyed everything which was good, beautiful and holy and lived by the power of violence, or do they want to imbibe the qualities of Ram, who believed in the equality of all, who gave up all riches and honors of the world because he thought his bother deserved the throne more than him? Whatever the West says, which is obsessed with China, India, a vibrant, English speaking, pro-western democracy is going to become the superpower of the 21st century. Do Indian Muslims want to participate in that great adventure ? Do they want to feel that they are part of India, that they are Indians? Nowadays it is politically not correct to say anything against Islam. You are immediately labeled anti-Muslim and dismissed as a "rightist". No matter if you are only reporting the fact that there is a real problem with Islam in South Asia: that India is surrounded by fundamentalists sates: Afghanistan, even after the fall of the Taliban, and Pakistan, while more moderates like Bangladesh, tend to close an eye to anti-Indian activities; that Indian Muslims sometimes tend to put their religion before their country; and that Kashmiris, far from being the persecuted that the Foreign Press likes to portray, are actually paying the price for having allowed Afghan and Pakistani Sunnis to radicalise what used to be a more gentle and tolerant

Islam and for leaving their Hindu brothers and sisters to be butchered and chased away from their ancestral land.

Thus the question has to be asked again: do Indian Muslims want to be like Babar or like Ram? This choice will shape their future for generations to come. The suicide attacks on the WTC and the Pentagon were a chilling reminder that even in the 21st century, some Muslims are ready to kill and get killed in the name of Allah. In this hour of tensions, it is time for Indian Muslims to understand that they have to be Indians first and Muslims second.

Ayodhya is the perfect example of the unwillingness of Indian Muslims to come to terms with the Indian reality; it is the symbol of a certain kind of insincerity and double standards.

Why Ayodhya?

AYODHYA is not a haphazard, crazy, meaningless event. It is a symbol through which two conceptions of India are facing each other, and the outcome of this confrontation will shape this country's future for generations to come. Ayodhya is also a sign of the pressure put upon India to remain faithful to her soul, to retain the essential of Dharma, true Hinduism; to avoid falling in the trap of total Westernisation, which has already stifled so many collective souls in the developing world. India's intellectual elite, instead of lamenting on the "death of secularism in India", the "mortal blow to our democracy", should do some honest, serious introspection, and see what the whole thing leads to. Because, ultimately, the force of evolution, whether individual or collective, always gives through events a hint of things to come, or points a finger at what is wrong in a particular set of circumstances. What are the roots of Ayodhya then? What is the core problem that led to the explosion? WHY AYODHYA?

The Threats at the Hands of Indian Themselves

To put the problem in its barest equation - and it is always good to come back to the obvious - the Ayodhya confrontation is between a mosque, emblem of the Islamic faith, and a temple, symbol of the Hindu religion. So, ultimately, it has to do between the Muslim-Hindu divide. This we all know. But what is the root of this divide? The Muslim conquest in India started in the 7th century AD, and in the words of Sri Aurobindo, the great Indian sage and revolutionary: "It took place at a time when the vitality of ancient Indian life and culture after 2,000 years of activity and creation was already exhausted or very near exhaustion and needed a breathing space to rejuvenate itself." Although Sri Aurobindo felt that "the vast mass of the Muslims in this country were and are Indians by race", he adds, "the real problem introduced by the Muslim conquest is the struggle between two civilisations, one ancient and indigenous, the other medieval and brought in from outside... That which has rendered the problem indissoluble is the attachment of each to a powerful religion, the one militant and aggressive, the other spiritually tolerant and flexible"... Sri Aurobindo thus always felt that the increasing antagonism between Hindus and Muslims was a game the Britishers played to divide India so as to rule her better: "...Then came the British empire in India which recast the whole country into artificial provinces made for its own convenience. British rule did not unite these people, but on the contrary, India was deliberately split on the basis of the two-nation theory into future Pakistan and Hindustan."

Ah, we are coming to Pakistan, at last. Because, after all, is not Pakistan, a million more times than Ayodhya, the symbol of the great Hindu-Muslim divide? How can the Ayodhya tangle be solved when two great nations, which are two parts of the same soul, which are but a play of diversity of the same oneness, are divided?

If Muslims leaders in India were a little wiser, they would voluntarily surrender the disputed site, thereby proving their goodwill and putting to silence their critics. Thus, in one stroke they would win the goodwill and trust of the whole Hindu community, not only in India, but also throughout the world. But no, they sabotaged the recent Shankaracharya of Kanchi mediation efforts, refusing to allow a token puja on the undisputed land, whereas the VHP had compromised by agreeing not to do it on the disputed site. It is always a case of Hindu bending against Muslim hardline; this is why maybe there is so much anger today in some of the Hindu lower classes against the Muslims. And unfortunately this anger erupted in the most horrible manner in Gujurat after the burning of the kar sevaks in the Sabamarti Express.

So let's phrase the question again: why Ayodhya? Well, Ayodhya is a sure sign that India and Pakistan (and also Bangladesh) must find ways to reunite, in any way, under any form, even a loose confederation, where everyone will keep its own identity, its own culture and religion. Then Ayodhya will only be a word in history books; then there will be no need to construct a mosque alongside a temple, or devise complicated and flimsy compromises that satisfy nobody in the end. Then there will be no more the Great Divide between Muslims and Hindus. Then even the Kashmir problem will get solved by itself. Then India will once again be the Greater India, Mother India, spiritual leader of the whole world.

Macaulay's Children

Why should Hindus not be proud of Hinduism? It has not only shaped the psyches of Hindus, but also of Indian Christians, Jains, Parsis, even Muslims, who are like no other Muslims in the world. And why should Indians be ashamed of their own civilisation whose greatness was foremost Hindu? Why should they refuse to have their children read the Vedas, which constitute one of the great fountains of spiritual wisdom, or the Bhagavad Gita, which contains all the secrets of eternal life? Or the Ramanaya and the Mahabharata, which teach the great values of human nature: courage, selflessness, spiritual endeavour, love of one's wife and neighbours.

Are the French ashamed of their Greco-Roman inheritance? Not at all ! On the contrary they even think that civilisation started only with the Greeks. Would you call the Germans or the Italians "nationalists" because they have Christian Democrats Parties? Christianity is the founding stone of Western civilisation and nobody dares deny it. American Presidents openly go to Church and swear on the Bible and no one finds anything to say. We French are brought-up listening to the values of Homer's "Iliad", or Corneille's "Le Cid". It is true that in France there has been a separation of the State and the Church; but that is because at one time the Church misused its enormous political power and grabbed huge amounts of lands and gold. But no such thing ever happened in India. The much maligned Brahmins never interfered in politics and today they are often a neglected lot.

Yet, educated Indians seem to suffer from an inferiority complex vis à vis the West. Do they think theirs is a lesser democracy, afflicted with all the world's ills? Does India's elite look down upon its own country?

To a Westerner, it seems very much so. India's upper class, the cream of this nation, the privileged, those very men and women who had the great fortune not to be born in need, appear to enjoy India-bashing. Nothing seems to find grace in their eyes: everything is rotten, the system, the government, the politicians, the bureaucracy. Nothing works, nothing is possible, everything is bleak, worthless, hopeless.

But the truth is that those Indians who constantly negate India, are ashamed of their country. Educated Indians always seem to compare their democracy to Western standards. Their parameters appear to be set by what the West thinks about India, by Amnesty International's comments on their nation. They want to apply to India the same norms which are used in the industrialised world. And extraordinarily, many of India's elite ridicule what makes this country unique in the world, what no other nation in the word possesses: Dharma, true Hinduism; the knowledge passed down by thousands of sages, saints, yogis, sadhus of the Eternal Truth, that which gives a meaning to this otherwise senseless life and which the West has totally lost: the Wheel of Life, the endless rebirths and ultimately the evolutionary Ascension of man towards the Ultimate Truth.

Do not Indians realise that by constantly belittling their own country and seeing it the way the West wants them to perceive it, they are handing over India to her enemies, those who wish her ill? Those who would like to see her humbled, broken, fragmented? Do these people want to see India go the way of Yugoslavia? Don't they realise that they are traitors to their own country, to its uniqueness, to is unparalleled greatness? That ultimately their India-bashing is a colonial leftover? An unconscious inferiority complex, which has been planted in the minds of their ancestors more than two centuries ago?

Nobody in India is more representative of this Hindu-bashing syndrome than some of the Indian Press. They whipped up the Ayodhya controversy time and again, forcing recently, even as the Shankaracharya of Kanchi had offered his mediation, the Congress and the Muslim leadership to make a stand against the performing of a puja on the undisputed site. It is they who label Hindus as Nazis fundamentalists, it is they who called Advani a Hitler (do they have any knowledge of European history: Hitler killed in cold blood 6 millions Jews and crores of other people). It is they who in the aftermath of the destruction shouted themselves hoarse over "the end of our secularism" or "the mortal blow to our democracy", forgetting in the heat of their self-righteousness that Ayodhya was a symbol. It is they who are still at it today, by portraying the Christian community in India as persecuted, when many of the incidents are the result of jealousies between converted and non-converted tribals, or are even engineered by Muslims and forgetting how much harm Christianity has done to this country for three centuries, converting by devious means, crucifying Brahmins in Goa, destroying temples in Pondichery...

True, the Indian Press should also be praised for its incredible diversity, for its inexhaustible reserve of talented writers, for its investigative journalism which makes sense when it helps uncover corruption, injustice, or political despotism. But again, it should learn to look at things NOT through the Western prism, but through the Indian looking glass, and apply to India standards that are Her own and of which she has nothing to be ashamed, because they are unique in the world.

Mother Theresa

I am born a Christian and I have had a strong Catholic education. I do believe that Christ was an incarnation of Pure Love and that His Presence still radiates in the world. I also believe that there are human beings who sincerely try to incarnate the ideals of Jesus and that you can find today in India a few missionaries (such as Father Ceyrac, a French Jesuit, who works mostly with lepers in Tamil Nadu), who are incarnations of that Love, tending tirelessly to people, without trying to convert them. But I also do believe that it is wrong to mix charity with conversion.

It is true that Christians are a much quieter force than the Muslims. They do not advocate openly the breaking-up of India, and certainly the great majority of Catholics in India are peaceful Indian citizens. Yet the missionary spirit brought in by the British is still alive in India and goes on quietly about its work, as Arun Shourie demonstrated in his book, "Missionaries in India" and as the continuing conversions of low-caste Hindus show clearly. And nothing symbolises this spirit better than Mother Theresa, even after her death.

But firstly, one should say in defence of Mother Theresa that she certainly did saintly work. After all, there is no denying that it takes a Westerner to pick-up the dying in the streets of Calcutta and raise abandoned orphans, a thankless task if there is one. Indian themselves, and particularly the Hindus, even though their religion has taught them compassion for 4000 years, have become very callous towards their less fortunate brethren and there are not enough Hindu organisations performing charitable work as the Christians do, although there is growing awareness amongst Hindu organisations that it's time to put their act together.

This said, one can wonder: what did Mother Theresa really stand for? Was caring for the dying and orphaned children her only goal ? Well, if you have observed her carefully over the years, you will notice that she did not say much. She did speak against contraception and abortion, in a country of more than one billion, where an ever growing population is swallowing whatever little economic progress is made; where the masses make life in India more and more miserable, invading the cities, crowding their streets and polluting their environments; where for 30 years the Indian Government has directed a courageous and democratic birth control programme, (whereas in China demographic control has achieved though autocratic means). She has also been attacked "for being a friend of the despots and accepting their money". But of course, many Indian intellectuals immediately sprang-up to the defence of Mother Theresa, saying it was "bad faith, bad taste", to speak thus. But still, the question may be asked : 1) what did Mother Theresa really stand for? 2) Why do Indians defend her so ardently?

The Threats at the Hands of Indian Themselves

During her whole lifetime, Mother Theresa spoke only of the dying of the streets in Calcutta, of the poor of India left unattended, of the miseries of the cities. Fair enough, but then it should have been pointed out to her, that she projected (and is still projecting today after her death, through the order she has created) to the whole world an image of India which is entirely negative: of poverty beyond humanity, of a society which abandons its children, of dying without dignity. OK, there is some truth in it. But then it may be asked again: did Mother Theresa ever attempt to counterbalance this negative image of India, of which she is the vector, by a more positive one? After all, she has lived here so long, that she knows the country as well as any Indian, having even adopted Indian nationality. Surely she can defend her own country? She could, for example, speak about India's infinite spirituality, her exquisite culture, the gentleness of its people, the brilliance of its children.

Unfortunately, Mother Theresa said nothing. For the truth is that she stood for the most orthodox Christian conservatism. There is no doubt that ultimately Mother Theresa's goal was utterly simple: to convert India to Christianity, the only true religion in her eyes.

Did you notice that she never once said a good word about Hinduism, which after all is the religion of 850 millions people of the country she said she loved and has been their religion for 5000 years. This is because deep inside her, Mother Theresa considered, as all good Christians do, particularly the conservatives ones, that Hinduism is a pagan religion which adores a multitude of heathen gods and should be eliminated.

For, make no mistake about it, there have been no changes about Christian or Protestant designs on India since they arrived with the Portuguese and the British, remember what Lords Hastings had to say about the Hindus! Mother Theresa was much more clever than Lord Hastings; she knew that on the eve of the 21st century, it would have looked very bad if she had openly stated her true opinions about Hinduism; so she kept quiet. But ultimately is not charitable work, whatever its dedication, a roundabout manner to convert people? For without any doubt, most of the people she saved from the streets did ultimately become Christians. And if you ask those "elite" Indians who knew her well, such as photographer Ragu Rai, a great admirer of her, she always came out after some years with : "It is now time for you to embrace the true religion". (Rai politely declined). This proselytising is unfortunately not over: now that Mother Teresa is in the process of being made a saint, her name will be further used to convert innocent villagers and tribals. Even in death, her "work" continues.

The "persecution" of Christians

Christianity has always striven on the myth of persecution, which in turn bred "martyrs" and saints, indispensable to the propagation of Christianity. But it is little known, for instance, that the first "saints" of Christianity, "martyred" in Rome, a highly refined civilization, which had evolved a remarkable system of gods and goddesses, some of whom were derived from Hindu mythology via the Greeks, were actually killed (a normal practice in those days), while bullying peaceful Romans to embrace the "true" religion, in the same way that later Christian missionaries would browbeat "heathen" Hindus, adoring many Gods, into believing that Jesus was the only "true" God.

Now to come to the recent cases of persecution of Christians in India at the hands of Hindu groups, I have personally investigated quite a few, amongst them the rape of the four nuns in Jhabua (MP), in 1999. This rape is still quoted as an example of the "atrocities" committed by Hindus on Christians. Yet, when I interviewed the four innocent nuns, they themselves admitted, along with George Anatil, Bishop

The Threats at the Hands of Indian Themselves 113

of Indore, that it had nothing to do with religion: it was the doing of a gang of Bhil tribals, known to perpetrate this kind of hateful acts on their own women. Today, the Indian Press, the Christian hierarchy and the politicians, continue to include the Jhabua rape in the list of the atrocities against the Christians. Or take the burning of churches in Andhra Pradesh in 2000, which was supposed to have been committed by the "fanatic" RSS. It was proved later that it was actually the handiwork of Indian Muslims, at the behest of the ISI, to foment hatred between Christians and Hindus. Yet the Indian Press, which went beserk at the time of the burnings, mostly kept quiet when the true nature of the perpetrators was revealed. Finally, even if Dara Singh does belong to the Bajrang Dal, it is doubtful if the 100 others accused do. What is more probable, is that like in many other "backward" places, it is a case of converted tribals versus non-converted tribals, of pent-up jealousies, of old village feuds and land disputes. It is also an outcome of what - it should be said - are the aggressive methods of the Pentecost and Seventh Day Adventist missionaries, known for their muscular ways of converting.

Thirdly, conversions in India by Christian missionaries of low caste Hindus and tribals are sometimes nothing short of fraudulent and shameful. American missionaries are investing huge amounts of money in India, which come from donation drives in the United States where gullible Americans think the dollars they are giving go towards uplifting "poor and uneducated Indians". It is common in Kerala, for instance, particularly in the poor coastal districts, to have "miracle boxes" put in local churches: the gullible villager writes out a paper mentioning his wish: a fishing boat, a loan for a pukka house, fees for the son's schooling. And lo, a few weeks later, the miracle happens! And of course the whole family converts, making others in the village follow suit.

American missionaries (and their Government) would like us to believe that democracy includes the freedom to convert by any means. But France for example, a traditionally Christian country, has a Minister who is in charge of hunting down "sects". And by sects, it is meant anything that does not fall within the recognised family of Christianity – even the Church of Scientology, favored by some Hollywood stars such as Tom Cruise or John Travolta, is ruthlessly hounded. And look at what the Americans did to the Osho movement in Arizona, or how innocent children and women were burnt down by the FBI (with the assistance of the US army) in Waco Texas, because they belonged to a dangerous sect.

Did you know that Christianity is dying in the West? Not only is church attendance falling dramatically because spirituality has deserted it, but less and less, youth find the vocation to become priests or nuns. And as a result, say in the rural parts of France, you will find only one priest for six or seven villages, whereas till the late seventies the smallest hamlet had its own parish priest. And where is Christianity finding new priests today? In the Third World, of course! And India, because of the innate impulsion of its people towards God, is a very fertile recruiting ground for the Church, particularly in Kerala and Tamil Nadu. Hence the huge attention that India is getting from the United States, Australia, or England and the massive conversion drive going on today.

It is sad that Indians, once converted, specially the priests and nuns, tend to turn against their own country and help in the conversion drive. There are very few "White" missionnaries left in India and most of the conversions are done today by Indian priests. Last year, during the bishop's conference in Bangalore, it was restated by bishops and priests from all over India, that conversion is the FIRST priority of the Church here. But are the priests and bishops aware that they would never find in any western country the same freedom to convert that they take for granted in India? Do they know that in China they would be expelled, if not put into jail? Do they realise that they have been honored guests in this country

The Threats at the Hands of Indian Themselves

for nearly two thousand years and that they are betraying those that gave them peace and freedom?

Hinduism, the religion of tolerance, the potential spirituality of this new millenium, has survived the unspeakable barbarism of wave after wave of Muslim invasions, the insidious onslaught of Western colonialism which has killed the spirit of so may Third World countries and the soul-stifling assault of Nehruvianism. But will it survive the present Christian offensive? Many Hindu religious leaders feel that Christianity is a real threat today, as in numerous ways it is similar to Hinduism, from which Christ borrowed so many concepts (see Sri Sri Ravi Shankar's book: " Hinduism and Christianity"). It is thus necessary that Indians themselves become more aware of the danger their culture and unique civilisation is facing at the hands of missionaries sponsored by foreign money. It is also necessary that they stop listening to the Marxist influenced English newspapers' defence of the right of Christian missionaries to convert innocent Hindus. Conversion belongs to the times of colonialism. We have entered the era of Unity, of coming together, of tolerance and accepting each other as we are – not of converting in the name of one elusive "true" God. When Christianity will accept the right of other people to follow their own beliefs and creeds, only then will Jesus Christ's Spirit truly radiate in the world.

Chapter 13

The Threats From India's Neighbours

For 40 years, India did not have relations with Israel. Yet, India and Israel share so much in common and both can learn a lot from each other! Hindus and Jews, far from being the persecutors of minorities that the Marxist, Arab and INC lobby like to portray, have been persecuted for nearly two thousand years and have been the victims of the two worst genocides in the sad history of humanity: Hitler, in his monstrous quest for a "pure" Aryan race, murdered six millions Jews in his gas chambers during the Second World War; and Belgium historian Koenraad Elst estimates that Hindus probably suffered the biggest holocaust in the whole history of our planet at the hands of Muslim invaders.

Indians and Israelis of today also share in common an awesome problem with Muslim fundamentalists. And India should learn a lesson or two from the way Israel handles this trouble, however much it is criticised by the western media. Unlike India, which since Independence has chosen to deal with this problem in the Gandhian spirit, that is by compromising most of the time with Islamic intransigence - if not giving in - Israel showed that toughness first, accompanied later by negotiations is much more productive, even if it pays today a heavy toll with the human havoc created by suicide bombers. Basically, the "land for money" concept is something that India should learn from : in 1967, Israel was threatened to be engulfed by its fanatic neighbors, so it stole the initiative by crushing them in a lightning six days war and kept some land which it used later as bargaining chips with Egypt and Syria. India is also surrounded by hostile Muslim countries: Pakistan, Afghanistan, and, more and more, Bangladesh. So far, India has followed the Nehruvian policy of Good Neighbourhood : you give first, expecting that your neighbour will reciprocate the gesture later. Unfortunately, history has shown that India mostly gets stabbed in the back for its generosity by small insignificant nations, such as Bangladesh, which owes its freedom thanks to the sacrifices of India's soldiers and is more and more lending its territory to the ISI. If during the 1965 Indo-Pak war, India would have kept a chunk of the Pakistani territory it has conquered, or if during the Kargil war, it had carried on with its victorious momentum by seizing some of Pakistan-held Kashmir, which could be used as a buffer zone, there would be probably today less cross-border terrorism.

Pakistan

1. India sees the Pakistan "hand" everywhere, whether it is the attack on Parliament in December 2001, or the burning of the kar sevaks in Godhra. Is Pakistan actually the continuing incarnation of those Muslim invaders who raped India from the middle of the 7th century onwards? Militant Hindus contend that nothing has changed: "their cry is still the same: "Dar-ul-Islam", the house of Islam. Yesterday they used scimitars, today they have the atomic bomb; but the purpose is identical, only the weapons have evolved: to conquer India, to finish what the Mughal Emperors were not able to achieve". To reason with Pakistan is useless, they conclude, "for once again they are only putting in practice what their religion teaches them every day that "the pagans shall burn forever in the fire of hell. They are the meanest of creatures". Or "Slay the infidels, wherever ye find them and take them captive

The Threats From India's Neighbours

and besiege them and prepare them for all kinds of ambush". Or again: "Choose not thy friends among the Infidels till they forsake their homes and the way of idolatry. If they return to paganism then take them whenever you find them and kill them". All these quotations are taken from the Koran and are read everyday to the faithful by their mollahs.(Koran 98:51-9:5-4:89).

Is Pakistan's war against India then a Muslim "jihad", the ultimate jihad against the Infidel, which if necessary will utilise the ultimate weapon, nuclear bombs? And as in the case of Ayodhya, the whole of Islam might side with Pakistan, for to their eyes India is still the Infidel, the Idolater, which the Koran asks them to slay. Says Elst: "if tomorrow the Pakistani start the Prophet's first nuclear war against an Infidel country (India), a billion Muslims will feel compelled to side with this muhajid struggle and dissenters will be careful not to protest aloud."

But then you also have to understand the Pakistani point of view: take Kashmir for instance. If one goes by the logic of Partition, then at least the Kashmir valley, which is in great majority Muslim, (and it should be emphasised that for a long time the Hindu Pandits in Kashmir exploited and dominated the Muslims -who are getting back at them today), should have reverted to Pakistan. It should be clear also that Pakistan never forgot the humiliating loss of Bangladesh at the hands of India, although India only helped Bangladesh to gain its freedom in the face of what the Bangladeshis say was Pakistani genocide. Zia's emergence was a result of that humiliation and the whole policy of proxy war by supporting the separatist movements in Punjab and Kashmir, is a way of getting back at India. And the same can be said about the nuclear bomb, for Pakistan has realised, after having lost three wars (four if you count Kargil), that both numerically and strategically, it can never beat India in a conventional conflict.

It is also clear when one goes to Pakistan today, that the country has evolved a soul of its own, has its individual identity and that in fact it has been able to do better than India in many fields. Their politicians are more accessible than in India for instance; their bureaucrats more friendly; and PIA is definitely a better airline than Indian Airlines! Finally, can Pakistanis be accused of all ills that befall India? The Indian Press has become possessed of total paranoia when it comes to Pakistan and Kashmir, always pointing a finger at its neighbour. But many of India's problems are of her own making

Thus, Indians can cry themselves hoarse about Pakistani treachery and see the evil hand of Islamabad everywhere, even sometimes behind events where Pakistan is not involved. But then the Indian Government should only blame themselves. For have they not recognised at independence the geographical and political reality of Partition and have they not continued to do so up to now? Is there any political leader in India who dares say today that India and Pakistan are ONE (except Mr Advani)? Is there any voice to proclaim the truth in a loud and clear voice, as Sri Aurobindo did in 1947: "But the old communal division into Hindu and Muslim seems to have hardened into the figure of a permanent division of the country. It is hoped that the Congress and the nation will not accept the settled fact as for ever settled, or as anything more than a temporary expedient. For if it lasts, India may be seriously weakened, even crippled: civil strife may remain always possible; possible even a new invasion and foreign conquest. THE PARTITION OF THE COUNTRY MUST GO"...

The menace from within cannot be tackled unless the menace from without is solved. India and Pakistan (and Bangladesh) are ONE. And as long as Partition remains, India will not be able to live in peace: Ayodhya, Kashmir, Kargil, Bangladeshi infiltration and a potential (nuclear?) war with Pakistan, are always possible.

The Threats From India's Neighbours

The Other Neighbours

How is it that India is almost universally disliked - sometimes even hated - by her neighbours, whether they are Muslim Bangladeshis, Buddhist Sri Lankans, or even Hindu Nepalese?

Journalists, both in South Asia, as well as in India, are fond of saying that it is because India is a great bully, with a "big brother", hegemonistic attitude. But in her past history, as we have seen, India has never shown any hegemonistic inclinations, her religion never tried to convert anybody and her armies never marched into other countries - the same cannot be said about Islam, or Christianity with her Crusades, or even the more peaceful Buddhist missionaries. Yet at one time India's influence, solely due to the sheer greatness of her culture and Hindu dharma, extended as far as China on one side and on Iran, Greece and even Europe on the other. Even today, whether in Thailand, Mauritius, Cambodia, or even Bangladesh and Pakistan, there is a tremendous leftover of India's predominance.

The key word must be fear. All these countries are afraid of India, not entirely because they think she is a great bully, but also because they unconsciously realise that they all sprang from India's vast bosom - and that one day, sooner or later, they might very well all return to that bosom, under whatever form. Nepal is a very good example of that India-hate syndrome. Here is a wonderful country, with simple and friendly people, which is the only Hindu nation in the world, which is so similar in many ways to India, that there is no reason to be antagonistic to a country with which it has so much in common. Yet before his assassination by his own son in 2001, King Birendra was often able to play a divide and rule game by using the Chinese and blaming India for all the ills of his country. Nepal has also become a haven for Pakistani agents, as the hijacking of the Indian Airlines flight in December 1999 showed. The same goes for Bangladesh. Bangladeshis, it is often said, are Bangladeshis first and Muslims second; this is why they separated from Pakistan, where they were treated as second-class citizens. And in truth, Bangladeshis are generally a friendly race, affectionate as all Bengalis, poetic, humorous. Their society used to be - and still is in many ways - one of the most open and tolerant in the world of Islam, which gives its women a unique place. Yet President Ershad was able to Islamise in a radical way this nation which stood proud of its secular history. Yet every time there is a flood, the Bangladeshis blame India and not the corruption of their own Government and their habit of living off the formidable funds they constantly get from aid agencies. Yet, a Taslima Nasreen, whatever her personal failings (love of publicity, inflated ego, unnecessary shocking of Islamic feelings), when she dares in her book "Lajja", to utter the truth about the atrocities perpetrated on Hindus after the destruction of the Ayodhya mosque, is hunted down by obscure fundamentalist groups, let down by her government, betrayed by her own people.

Same phenomenon in Sri Lanka. Extraordinary country the erstwhile Ceylon; God gave it everything: exceptional climate, lush country, incredible diversity of races and religions, an easy-going and friendly people, who even welcomed its invaders. Yet the hate that the Sinhalese have for Indians is something to be seen to be believed. Again it is a hate which was fostered by their political leaders: the late President Premadasa became adept at using the hate-India carrot every time he was in trouble. He also tried to utilise the LTTE too many times, sometimes killing them, sometimes wooing them - and got assassinated in the process. And why should India be blamed for Sri Lanka's ills?

India has also to account for the hostility of the Gulf countries. And very unfortunately, India's hands are bound, because of its millions of nationals, most of them Muslims,

The Threats From India's Neighbours

who work in the Gulf and regularly send home precious foreign exchange (even if this tendency is nowadays decreasing). But does India realise that this foreign exchange is sometimes a poisoned gift, that these Indian Muslims often bring home a more militant Islam? The Bombay blasts which followed the destruction of the Babri Masjid were the perfect example of that threat to India from the Gulf countries. Not only did the Indian Muslims, who were the hands that executed, receive training, arms and financing from Pakistan, but some of the Gulf countries must have had a prior knowledge of them. The fact that the perpetrators were able to transit through two of these Gulf countries after their deed is proof enough: the police of these countries are everywhere and are totalitarian tools to the monarchies; they must have known when the Memons entered the country and exactly where they were staying. It would have been a simple matter to stop them from leaving both the countries till an extradition was officially asked for. Yet they chose to let them go and now "Tiger" Memon has gone into hiding in Pakistan and India will probably never see him again and solve the mystery of the Bombay blasts. Why did Dubai and Jeddah let him go? And why did the Indian Government do nothing to prevent it? The madrasas and the Sunni rigid fundamentalism which have crept in places like Godhra in Gujarat, are also directly responsible for such terrible acts as the burning of the kar sevaks in the Sabamarti Express by a crowd of Muslims led by Muslim Congress municipal counsellors.

One has to understand the Arab psyche: by destroying the Ayodhya mosque, it is the whole Muslim world which secretly or overtly has felt insulted and humiliated. Furthermore, none of the Gulf countries have forgotten India's support to Iraq during the Gulf war. IS IT POSSIBLE THEN THAT IT WAS DECIDED TO TEACH INDIA A LESSON? That Pakistan and "some" other Muslim countries funded and planned, or at least knew in advance, of the Bombay bombings, which were followed by the Coimbatore attempt on LK Advani, the car bombing of the Srinagar Parlimanet in 2001, or the terrorist attack on the Indian Parliament in New Delhi in December 2001 and the 22nd January 2002 attack on the American Cultural Centre in Calcutta ? Is this a warning of the Muslim world to Hindu India? But who are the fundamentalists? Who are the murderers? Who are the Nazis? Who are the Hitlers?

China

It is the infamous 1972 "historical trip" of Richard Nixon to Peking which set the trend: henceforth, the West was gradually going to put all its chips on the Chinese, banking that one day, its investments, political and economical, will bring enormous returns. In the process, the West conveniently forgot that the Chinese had killed 1,2 million Tibetans, one of the worst genocides of humanity. Tianamen showed again openly the totalitarian face of Chinese communism, but the United States preferred to forget it as fast as possible; today it is the inhuman crackdown on the Falun Gong, harmless people, whose only crime is to meditate, exercise and protest non violently. The Chinese, clever as they are, make, from time to time, a few Human Rights concessions here and there, such as releasing a handful of dissident student leaders (who by the way, have never raised their voices against the Tibetan genocide), or letting go of the crew of the American spy plane, and at the same time they harden their tone. Washington pretends to be satisfied and gives again the green light to its army of businessmen, waiting impatiently to place their green dollars in the huge Chinese slot machine.

But is the West ready to pay the price for that impatience? Because finally, economical liberalisation or not, China remains a communist country with a dictatorial leadership, probably the only one worth that name left in the world. And communism means instability, as the sudden crumbling of the Soviet Union and Eastern Europe, has proved. What is going to happen to the billions of dollars of Western investment, if there is tomorrow a counter-revolution in China - or if communism shows again its true totalitarian face?

Russia's back is broken and it is no more a danger to China and it is thus towards North Indian cities that most of China's nuclear missiles are pointed. This raises several important questions. India in her generosity, (through Jawarlhal Nehru), welcomed the Dalaï-Lama and his followers in 1959 and allowed them to settle in Dharamsala where, thanks to their spiritual leader's guidance, the Tibetans were able to recreate a small Tibet, complete with Government in exile, schools, monasteries, Tibetan medicine and arts. It is actually the only real thing that is left of Tibetan culture and civilisation today and if the Tibetans ever recover Tibet, it will have to be re-transplanted to what has become a near completely Chinese Tibet.

But the Chinese have never forgiven India for their generosity and compassion towards the Tibetans. And although some progress has been made and the External Affairs Minister, Jaswant Singh, has just opened the first direct air link between India and China, the question remains: can Indians trust the Chinese?

There are two superpowers in the making in Asia: India and China. The West seems to have lost the absolute predominance it used to enjoy and with its slow decline, it will drag in recession many of the so-called tigers of Asia, which vitally need US and Western political support for the growth of their economy: after Tibet and Hong-Kong, it might soon be Taiwan which will be swallowed back by China. And ultimately India and China will be the only superpowers left with Japan in their shadow. But one will be a democratic country, and the other will still be a communist dictatorship, with a formidable military arsenal - nuclear and otherwise - at her disposal for her greedy appetite. China seems to be the direct adversary of India, both economically and militarily, and not Pakistan, as the Indian Government wants its citizens to believe.

The West

And finally, no chapter on the threat to India from without can be complete without a mention of the attitude of the Western world, particularly the United States. It is true that after the 11th September 2001 terrorist attacks on America, there has been a change in the way Washington looks at India; but nevertheless, India remains isolated in Asia and the fact that the US chose Pakistan as its frontline state for its war on terrorism tells it all.

"Target Humanity" titled the editorial of a national Indian daily, the day after the horrendous terrorist attacks on the United States. Did the honourable editor of that newspaper think that when the Americans are struck by Islamic terrorism, it is humanity which is targeted, and when Indians – Hindus rather – are struck, it is sub-humanity which is targeted?

It would seem so. Because, however dramatic, however enormous, however spectacular, however deadly in terms of human lives these attacks on the United States were, India has been the target of Islamic terrorism for decades, with the world not only taking no notice, but the United States also turning a blind eye to the perpetrators of these barbarous acts.

But if only it was the Western press which was biased against India! Indian journalists themselves have played a nefarious role: they have, for instance, recently devoted pages and pages to the "saffronisation" of India's education, whereas it is entirely justified for a country to teach its children about the greatness of its ancient civilisation; but when Islamic groups in Kashmir hurl acid on women to force them to wear the burqua, it is reported in most of Indian newspapers in a few lines, without any of the outrage shown against Dr Murali

The Threats From India's Neighbours

Manohar Joshi, who has not thrown any acid on innocent girls, nor killed anybody. The Indian Press has shown the same partiality during the recent conference on racism in South Africa. It chose to focus on the issue of the persecution of dalits in India, forgetting that India is one of the only countries in the world to have initiated a reservation policy for its underprivileged (does the US have a reservation policy for its poor Negroes?), that India's President is a dalit, which shows that here, someone born in a low caste can rise to the highest post, while in France for instance, a Jew will find it very difficult to become President, or that Krishna, India's most beloved God, was from a low caste, as are many Indian saints and sages. This whole conference was a sham and a shame, concentrating on Zionism as the worst form of racism, whereas, like India, Israel is fighting a life and death battle against Muslim fundamentalism.

These attacks are indeed terrible and we mourn the loss of human lives. But maybe they were necessary to wake-up the West to the reality of Islamic terrorism. Let us also not forget that the United States literally created the Taliban, by arming, training and unleashing Pakistani Islamic fundamentalism against the Soviets in Afghanistan. India has been fighting (with Russia and Israel) a very lonely battle against Muslim fundamentalism, which is a real threat to a free and democratic world. Hindus are not only hounded and killed in Kashmir, but also all over India in bomb attacks, be it in Kerala or in Delhi. Hindus are persecuted in Pakistan, in Bangladesh, in Afghanistan, in Fiji, all this not only in the midst of total indifference from the world community, but also on the part of the English speaking Indian Press. It is time now that the West, particularly the United States, understands that India is a bastion of pro-Western democracy in the midst of an Asia in the throes of a growing Islamic fundamentalism, from Kabul to Srinagar, from Karachi to Indonesia, from Chechnya to Sin-Kiang.

Once again, these terrorist attacks are terrible, but not only will they serve to jolt the West to the reality of Islamic terrorism, to which they have turned so often a blind eye (remember how an Egyptian pilot "suicided" his whole Egyptian Airlines 767 in 2000 and how it was hushed up for fear of "offending" America's Arab allies), but it is also a blessing in disguise for India. The BJP Government can now take strong measures against Islamic fundamentalism on its soil (but will they?) and it will have the support of the whole western community. Pakistan will be seen in its true light, as a supporter of international terrorism, and the only country in the world, with Saudi Arabia, which supports Afghanistan and Bin Laden; and the BJP can now silence the Congress and the Communists, which have been the main opponents to a radical change in India. Unfortunately the BJP does none of that.

Finally, Samuel Huntington was right: in his book "The Clash of Civilisations", he had predicted that the 21st century would see a battle between Islamic fundamentalism, with the sometimes covert support of China (as witnessed in Pakistan, who developed its nuclear bomb thanks to Chinese technology), on one side, and the West and India on the other side. What happened on the 11th of September 2001 is going to dramatically alter the political outlook of the West towards Islamic fundamentalism in general and towards India, in particular. Israel is going to come out of its political isolation (in greater part fostered by the media, such as the BBC, which portray the Palestinians as freedom fighters, in the same way that they paint the Chechnyans or Kashmris as heroes) and the Israelis as the bad guys. Even China is going to lose some of its lustre, as India is going to slowly become the West's privileged ally in Asia. It is also time for Indian journalism to wake-up and come out of its double standards, which are a direct inheritance of Macaulay's education: Hindus are also human.

Pokharan

Thanks to the atomic explosions in the Pokharan desert of 1998, India has today the nuclear bomb, but should India freeze her Integrated Missile Programme, under the pressure of the United States (as she seems to have already partially done)? Should India sign the CTBT and scrap her potential nuclear power and delivery clout?

All weapons of war are a perversion of man's greed and the ultimate symbol of the misuse he has achieved over matter. Thus, ideally, they should all be banned, or else slowly phased out until we all live in a weaponless world, for the simple reason that they would not be needed anymore and that man would have outgrown their folly.

Therefore, more than anything, the atom bomb symbolises that folly, because at a single stroke, at the simple push of one button by a misguided hand, or through the order of a mad leader, thousands of lives can be obliterated in a single second, entire cities be wiped out in a single flash.

The film, the Day After, has given us an inkling of that terror, a glimpse of that horror. The atom bomb also demonstrates the limit of man's command over matter. For what use is that material mastery to man, when he has no control over his impulses, when he is still unable not only to love his human brothers, but even to reason with himself not to use his domination over matter to harm others. And ultimately, his might may slip out of his hands, because material mastery without inner control is incomplete and dangerous.

For this and many other reasons, should not India then voluntarily forsake nuclear power and cap its missile programme and become a true non-violent country, in the spirit of the Mahatma Gandhi?

But have those who are pushing this theory forward read properly the Baghvad Gita? For once more, what does the Baghavad tell us? It does not say, as Christians do, or as the Mahatma purported, that all violence is wrong. It asserts that when violence is absolutely necessary, when it is used for defending one's country, one's wife, brothers, sisters, then it becomes Dharma - duty - and is acceptable, as long as it is done with the right attitude in one's heart.

India, as we have just seen, is facing multiple threats from without, by hostile nations armed with both conventional and atomic weapons. The Islamic bomb, assembled by Pakistan with Arab financing, is the first one of these.

The Indian Government also knows that many Chinese nuclear missiles are positioned on the Tibetan plateau and pointed towards North Indian cities. For this and many other reasons, India should for the moment develop its nuclear military programme, in spite of the increasing pressure from the West, particularly the United States. India needs again Kshatriyas to defend herself, not businessmen, or intellectuals who will sell their country for a few more million dollars investments and a pat on the back from Uncle Sam.

It is to be hoped that India will realise that surrendering to America's pressure would jeopardise her unity and open her for dismemberment. For her nuclear and missile programmes are not meant for aggression - once again in her 7000 year history, India was never an aggressor - but as a deterrent to protect herself, to show her enemies that she means business and that she will retaliate in case of first attack. It is a sad reality of the world today, and India has got to take it in to consideration. Let India be strong, powerful, nuclear even, but as dharma, because it is her duty to protect her children.

Chapter 14

The Hindus are also to blame

Hindus are also to blame for the ills that befell India in the last few centuries: the withdrawal from the world by its yogis, the neglect of Life and Matter, the terrible abuses done in the name of caste, the loss of the Kshatriya spirit, or the total lack of civic sense amongst Hindus, have all contributed to the sad state of India today.

Hindus.

Individually, Hindus are the most wonderful people in the world: full of hospitality, gentleness, innate spirituality. But whatever happened to the collective consciousness of the nation? The gap between the very rich and the extremely poor is constantly widening nowadays. If only the very fortunate would care for their less flourishing brethren, or the higher castes devote some of their time and resources to the Harijans. But it needed a Mother Theresa to remind us that the dirty work in India cannot be done by its own people. India is a vast dump of garbage, not because it is too poor to process it and store it properly, BUT BECAUSE IT DOES NOT CARE, BECAUSE THE INERTIA IN THIS COUNTRY IS SO VAST, SO DEEPLY INGRAINED IN THE COLLECTIVE CONSCIOUSNESS, THAT NOBODY GIVES A DAMN FOR THE OTHER.

Indians show also very little civic sense in other domains of their life. Look how they drive. Truck and bus drivers in India routinely overtake on curves, endangering not only their passengers' lives but also those of oncoming traffic. They park most of the time in the middle of the road when they have to stop, without any concern for those who are coming behind. They drive us deaf in Delhi with their constant blaring horns and generally have a total disregard for others. And does not the way one drives, show a nation's vital soul? When an Israeli, who said that everything happens in his country with guts, asked his Indian counterpart how it was done in India, he was told: with luck! Look also at how Indians are in the habit of pushing other people, whether it is to enter a bus, or exit a cinema. Or how they so innocently ignore those who have been queuing for hours at some railway counter, by jumping to the head of the queue. And it is not only the poor, but also the rich, who have this habit; witness the checking-in at airports.

Dishonesty is also a lack of collective discipline. Glimpse how the Indian man is often cheating, whether it is the contractor mixing cement with ashes, the change not tendered exactly, or the affluent man (ex:cricketers, ministers) who swindles the income tax, by keeping crores of black money, gold and jewels in his house, when he could very well afford to pay a little more tax and put his money in his bank? It is said that in this way one third of India's wealth is in the black. For make no mistakes, India is a wealthy country. The poverty is only there because of the mismanagement, the dishonesty, the tamas and the inheritance of wrong structures. For Indians must be, with the Jews, the best savers in the world. And they don't save in abstract concepts: they go in for solid gold, land, cash - and that from the little shopkeeper to the business magnate. Where is all this money going? Again, through a lack of discipline, lack of concern for the nation and disregard for what one's egoism will do to the country.

Politicians

And what about politicians? Nowadays, Indian politicians have often become a caricature, which is made fun of by the whole country. Even the BJP, in which so many Hindus had high hopes, showed that, once in power, its politicians succumb to the same weaknesses as the politicians from the other parties.

"Spirituality is India's only politics, the fulfilment of Sanatana Dharma its only Swaraj", wrote Sri Aurobindo in 1911 (India's rebirth,89). Today we see corrupt, inefficient men, who have lost track of the good of the nation they are supposed to serve, who are only interested in minting the maximum money in the minimum time. Some of the BJP's ministers, such as Murali Manohar Joshi, whatever his shortcomings, have shown that the ancient notion of seva, selfless work for the nation, can still be revived. India should adopt a Presidential system, where the President can chose his ministers, who will not necessarily be MPs.

And what about the habit of Indian politicians of declaring holidays at the drop of the hat ? India must be the place in the world where there are the most samadhis, where each year, enormous amounts of time and money are wasted to celebrate the death anniversaries of people which have been completely forgotten and who often did not achieve anything worthwhile in their lifetimes. Five minutes of silence in all offices should be enough to pay respect to the memory of any important figure who dies. In Madhya Pradesh for example, it has been calculated that there are more leave days (holidays, strikes, bandhs, leave), than working days!

There is also nothing which better symbolises the degeneration of Indian politicians than the VIP syndrome. The protection that most politicians enjoy today was born out of the trauma of seeing Indira Gandhi killed by her own bodyguards and Rajiv Gandhi by a human bomb; it sprang from a sincere desire to protect future Indian VIPs from such a fate. But once again perversion has taken over, and man, the political animal, has misused what was in the beginning a genuine movement. Today, no leader in the world, even the President of the United Sates, is as protected as the Indian

Prime Minister. France, which has its fair share of Islamic fundamentalism - there have been numerous deadly attacks against its railways, shopping plazas, airlines even - has learnt to cope with security in an efficient and discreet manner. President Chirac, for instance, does not move around with an army of rude and brutish security men; and one still remembers how Francois Mitterrand, the previous President, used to go out at night to his favourite restaurant with only two bodyguards.

Everything has already been said about the hassles that VIP security has created in India: the status symbol it has become for people like Mulayam Singh, who are not particularly targeted by terrorists; how 70% of the Indian police is tied-up by VIP protection, instead of attending to the problems of its common citizens; how we all suffer at the hands of VIP's, waiting endlessly in our cars as the Honourable Sonia Gandhi passes by, or in planes as the PM's aircraft is landing; or of being rudely treated by the arrogant and useless Black Cats, all of whom should be sent to guard Kargil in winter, so they get a taste of what real security is about. And what about the Indian Prime Ministers' and Presidents' habit of chartering a full jumbo jet from Air India for their travels abroad? And when a technical snag occurs, the PM finds it quite normal to requisition another one on the spot, throwing into disarray hundreds of passengers, including many foreigners, as Air India's planes have a round the clock schedule. Can the Prime Minister not have his own plane, even if its is more modest than a Jumbo jet? India, after all, is a poor country.

Politicians who are afraid of dying should remember what Krishna tells Arjuna in the the Bhagavad Gita: "the body is just an envelope and the soul never dies, but is born and reborn again to complete its works". Do they not know that if they are going to die tomorrow at the hands of an assassin, then it will be their karma, that it has been written somewhere in the book of destiny and that there is nothing that any security in the world, however sophisticated, can do about it? Remember how Ronald Reagan, the most protected man in the world, was shot; or how the LTTE always manages to get the Sinhalese and Tamil leaders it targets, although the Sri Lankans, being trained by the Israelis, have one of the best security forces in Asia? However good and wise a leader is – most of India's politicians are pretty old - and India being such a vast and ancient country, there will always be other "vibhoutis" to replace him if he were to be assassinated. So why fear death? Does India always have to ape the West, when it has such deep knowledge in itself of the reality beyond the reality, of the occult truth behind appearances? Does the present government not understand that if it would address itself seriously to the problems of VIP security and tone it down DRASTICALLY, including around the Prime Minister, it would acquire the party tremendous goodwill from the people and as many votes as wining the Kargil war?

And finally one has to quote again from the great Avatar of our era: "I have no doubt we shall have to go through our Parliamentary period in order to get rid of the notion of western democracy, by seeing in practice how helpless it is to make nations blessed... It is only when this foolishness is done with, that truth will have a chance to emerge and a really strong spiritual movement begin as a prelude to India's regeneration..." (India's rebirth, P.89).

And truly, India will get rid of her corrupt politicians; only when she accepts that she made a mistake by adapting blindly all the political structures which the British had put in place to govern this country; only when India starts experimenting with her own ancient systems, which have been adapted to today's problems, that an efficient and honest government will spring from her bosom, ready to do service to Mother India, in the old Kshatryia spirit. It is only when India will see through the shortcomings of democracy, that she will get rid of the bureaucrats who are eating up her entrails.

Sports

Another area where Indians have miserably failed is sports. One sees the energy of a nation in sports. And what happened in India? It thrives in sports inherited from the British, such as cricket, a game which is a colonial legacy, which is meant to be played in cool weather on a green English meadow with a few spectators who shout "jolly good" from time to time, while sipping lemonade. It is not a game intended for a tropical country where you stand for hours under a blistering sun with frenzied fans screaming their approval or displeasure. Cricket has become an obsession here and has totally vampirised all the other sports in India. There is so much money, sponsorship, television and even the Government has concentrated so much only on cricket, at the expense of all the other sports, that corruption and cheating have set in and a big scandal emerged when it was revealed that Cronje, the South African captain, had taken money from an Indian bookie to lose a match .

India is nowhere in the international arena of sports and its standard is pathetic if not ridiculous in all sports except for another two British legacies: tennis and hockey. But look at China, in the early eighties it also could not compete in any discipline, bar table tennis, but in a span of thirty years, it has become a sports superpower in all areas, even in some disciplines not suited to their morphology, such as swimming. Why can't India, the country that gave us hatha yoga, which has been copied the world over, or even pranayama, which is now spreading like wildfire all over the planet, have a coherent and comprehensive program which would build world-class athletes in two decades?

Because of cricket! And it is so unfair: athletes, such as long distance runners, will train in miserable conditions, get a pittance as sponsorship and often have to work full or part time in some obscure Government jobs. Compare this to cricketers who stay in five star hotels, get millions of rupees in sponsorship and advertisement, are often arrogant and still manage to lose most of the time!

The Indian Government should restrict the number of international matches played by Indian cricketers happening both within and outside India. This will ensure automatically that cricketers get less sponsorship and have to concentrate on home turf. And it should evolve a bold and clear plan for developing other sports, trying as much as possible to bypass bureaucracy which stifles and kills all the good plans (it would maybe make sense to privatise some of the areas such as training). Then only will India become a superpower in sports.

Is India's body going to waste ?

During the WTO negotiations, India wanted to de-link child labour from other issues. Although the West is right in pointing out that there is indeed a terrible exploitation of child labour in India, by people who make shameful money out of them: beedie factories owners, carpet makers, cracker factories etc., at the same time, child labour is a reality of India, which cannot be wished away, as many poor families depend on the earnings of their children to survive. And it is not for the West, which is itself disgracefully exploiting cheap labour in Third World countries, to give lessons to India.

On the other hand, one is a little surprised to hear India's various Commerce Ministers protest against the West's insistence to link trade with environmental safeguards and norms. It would be all right for the honorable Minister, to whichever party he belongs, to ride on his high horse of offended honor if India's ecology was in a good state. But the simple truth is that it is near the point of no return - and no government, be it the Congress or the BJP, has cared a hoot about India's environment, except to pay some lip service (and we have seen how the BJP made a political appointment out of the Ministry of Environment, showing how low India's ecology is on its agenda). But did they think for a moment that the Ministry of Environment may be as important as the Defense Ministry, because two nuclear bombs dropped by Pakistan on India will not do as much harm to India as fifty years of greedy saw-mill owners, in league with corrupt politicians and forest officers, have done to India's environment?

Because the truth is that by the middle of this century there will be no more forest cover left in India. Its population will have long crossed the billion and half mark and will overflow everywhere, stifling any progress, annihilating all efforts. India's cities will be so polluted by their millions of cars that it will be impossible to breathe any more. India's rivers will be so poisoned by industries, that all life will long have disappeared from them. There will be no drinking water left, except imported mineral water. And India will be littered with so much plastic (bags, bottles, buckets, etc.), that it will be materially impossible to ever get rid of them, (indeed the land of Bharat should be renamed "the civilisation of plastic"). This is 21st century India for you.

Many experts have already pointed out that hardly 11% of India's classified forests have adequate density. In 1950, 1/3 of India's area was still forested; each year India loses, through deforesting, a territory bigger than France, that is nearly two million hectares. And of these, only 3% is protected. And even that 3% is in deep distress, because of population pressure, big dams (like the Narmada), and industries. The Forest Department, which although it claims that it does selective tree felling, has absolutely no understanding of ecological balance.

But without doubt, the greatest culprits of the massive deforestation, the dwindling of animal life, the thinning of underwater tables and the increasing desertification of India, are the politicians, in connivance with the contractors, who

The Hindus are also to blame

in turn bribe the forest officers. Witness how Veerapan was able to plunder the forests of Tamil Nadu and Karnataka for ten years; today it is said that there is no sandalwood forest left in the South and that India has to start importing it from Australia. The Konkan railway, the Narmada Dam, the increase of the prawn farms, are all examples of these criminal wrongdoing. And unfortunately, but for Maneka Gandhi, who was the only serious Environment Minister India ever had, there have never been as many harmful projects to ecology as lately. Did you know for instance that the Asian Development Bank is funding a four-lane highway between Calcutta and Kanyakumari, called the "East Coast Road", which will create havoc with India's coast line? Already thousands of trees have been cut on the Mahabalipuram-Pondichery stretch; fields have been bulldosed; houses have been destroyed; entire villages sometimes are to be expropriated. How could the Central Government approve of a road so harmful to India's interests? Fortunately, there is a growing ecological awareness in India and movements led by Medha Patkar, Shri Baghuna, or the lawyer Mehta, are doing wonderful work. But they often stand alone because as long as the people of India are not educated, their work is doomed.

But ultimately, is it fair to blame only the politicians, or even the British, who started the massive deforestation for their railways and killed hundreds of thousands of tigers? Is there not something else in the Indian psyche that is to blame? Where is the root of this massive unconcern for one's environment; this total disregard for beauty, whether it is the terrible ugliness of the cities in Punjab, or the appalling filthiness in Tamil Nadu? And, maybe, for once, the Hindus are to blame. The Ganges seems to be the perfect illustration of a religion which enjoins a thousand purification rites and yet has allowed her own Mother earth to be defiled. Here is a river that Hindus have held most sacred for centuries, nay millenniums; to bathe in it is to purify oneself of all bad karma; to die here is to be reborn in Light. Yet what do all Hindus do with their sacred Ganges? They defecate in it; they throw in all their refuse; they let their dead float down the mighty river, AS IF THEY THOUGHT THAT THE SPIRITUAL PURITY OF THE WATER CAN NEVER BE OBLITERATED BY MATERIAL DIRTINESS. But ask any scientist what is the degree of pollution in the Ganges today and he will tell you that it is near the point of no return. What will happen to India if it loses the Ganges, which is its very soul?

So, for once, India should copy the West, which has grown a tremendous ecological concern and developed various ways of fighting against the physical degradation of our planet. We have seen, for instance, how India has been forced to adopt certain environmental measures just out of greed, when European countries refused to accept any textile export which was not ozone free, or leather which was chemically poisoned. Look how Auroville, the international city near Pondichery founded in 1968 by the Mother of the Sri Aurobindo Ashram, and where a 1000 people from 25 countries live together, has shown how fast the earth can be redeemed, even when the task looks hopeless. When the first settlers arrived, Auroville was a barren plateau of red earth, with no trees left, except a few palms and one or two banyans. Yet old temples still showed records of a once abundant land with forests and wildlife. But indiscriminate tree cutting and heavy monsoons washed away all the good topsoil into the sea, creating huge canyons and the water table had dropped extremely low. The early Aurovillians, mostly foreigners, first stopped the rain water from washing into the sea by erecting earth bunds wherever they could. Thus the water table slowly went up again. Then, they proceeded to plant a million trees, protecting them with thorns from goats and cows, which are a mortal danger to India's ecology. When these trees started growing, they shed their leaves which, with the help of rain water, started rotting on the ground, recreating in a few seasons a fertile topsoil. Today Auroville is a vast forest, animal life has come back,

The Hindus are also to blame   141

the canyons are slowly filling up, and villagers have so much firewood, that they do not cut trees any more. Yet these same villagers still keep on planting cashewnut crops, a harmful tree, which has to be sprayed many times with deadly pesticides and whose only value is its international market price. And these villagers still let rain water flow into the sea and use cheap compost, mixed with plastic bags, hospital refuse and other non-disposable trash. EDUCATION is the word; the Indian Government has got to educate its villagers on the value of the sacred land that is India. India is slowly killing its most precious possession, as no Muslim invader or European coloniser ever managed to do. Without its land, India will be like a great soul without a body, unable to manifest itself.

P.S. A word must be said about Aids, when talking about disasters. Aids seems to be the scourge of the 21st century, the great black plague of our era. Why the emergence of this sudden dreaded disease? Is it because man has gone against Nature in the last sixty years and Nature always has the last word? Is Aids the outcome of some secret genetic manipulation on monkeys for biological warfare purpose, which went wrong and spread in Africa before reaching Europe and the rest of the world? Nobody will probably ever know the truth.

World health organisations are very fond of saying that India has the greatest reservoir of HIV contaminated cases - some even speak about 10 million. But as every one knows, Aids spreads mainly by three means: homosexuality, hypodermic syringes of drug addicts and prostitutes. Yet homosexuality is not very common in India's villages, which comprise 80% of the population; one-sided homosexuality is a Western phenomenon and it is brought into India by Westernised Indians. As for drug addiction, again it is not common in Indian villages, except in the Eastern border states, of which incidentally many happen to be Christians. Thus remain the prostitutes who constitute the greatest threat of spreading the disease, particularly in big cities like Bombay. Then in turn, those men who have contracted it will bring it to the villages, when they have intercourse with their wives. Let us hope that once more India's Dharma will protect her from another threat, this one so insidious and deadly that it could create havoc among its youth.

Chapter 15

The Real India

Within.

It is not only the British education system which was blindly adopted at Independence by Nehru, but also the whole British judicial, constitutional, and legal set-up. The Constitution, for instance, has repeatedly shown its flaws, as the Presidents, who have no real powers, are playing more and more games and trying to impinge upon the Prime Minister's prerogatives. Democracy in India has also been perverted: we have seen how the Congress, who in the last three elections of the 20th century made disastrous showings, has used the subtleties of the system to bring down four successive governments, thus provoking useless and expensive elections, which in turn provided no stable governments until the National Democratic Alliance won by a landslide in 1999. Therefore, it is the whole democratic system of India that has to be reshaped to suit a new, truer nation, which will manifest again its ancient wisdom.

And what is true democracy for India, but the law of Dharma? It is this law that has to be revived, it is this law that must be the foundation of a true democratic India: "It has been said that democracy is based on the rights of man; it has been replied that it should rather take its stand on the duties of man; but both rights and duties are European ideas. Dharma is the Indian conception in which rights and duties lose the artificial antagonism created by a view of the world which makes selfishness the root of action and regain their deep and eternal unity. Dharma is the basis of democracy which Asia must recognise, for in this lies the distinction between the soul of Asia and the soul of Europe." (India's Reb p.37- March 16th 1908).

And the most wonderful thing is that, practically, India has at hand the model of a new form of democracy in the old Panchayat system of Indian villages, which has to be revived and worked up to the top. These ancient Panchayat systems and their guilds were very representative and they had a living contact with the people. On the other hand, the parliamentary system has lost contact with the masses: the MP elected from Tamil Nadu or Andhra Pradesh, sits most of his time in Delhi, an artificial, arrogant and faraway city. The palatial bungalow, the car, the servants, the sycophancy, the temptation to become corrupt he encounters there, make him forget his original aspiration to serve the people – if he ever had one. What has to be done is not only to decentralise the Government, by giving a greater autonomy to the states – which should take care of most separatist movements – but also to send back the elected politicians to their fields of work, so that they have a living contact with their people, as they did two thousand years ago : "We had a spontaneous and a free growth of communities developing on their own lines...Each such communal form of life - the village, the town, etc. - which formed the unit of national life, was left free in its own internal management. The central authority never interfered with it... because its function was not so much to legislate as to harmonise and see that everything was going all right"... (India's Rebirth 172).

The Judiciary, with its millions of backlog cases, which sometimes take decades to be decided upon, with its lawyers looking like crows in their ridiculous black dresses, would have to be reviewed too. The recent Supreme Court judgments on Ayodhya showed again the limits of the Western judicial

The Real India

system by having the arrogance to think three judges, with their own bias, could decide on something so ancient, so sacred and so complicated. It would be absurd to put the Manu law back into practice; but certainly the law of Dharma, of Truth, should be translated into a new judicial system. Not to judge according to Western standards, with its so-called secular values, which have no relevance to India : "The work of the legislators attempted to take up the ordinary life of man and of the community and the life of human desire and aim and interest and ordered rule and custom and to interpret and formulate it in the same complete and decisive manner and at the same time to throw the whole in to an ordered relation to the ruling ideas of the national culture and frame and perpetuate a social system intelligently fashioned so as to provide a basis, a structure, a gradation by which there could be a secure evolution of the life from the vital and mental, to the spiritual motive.." (Found of Indian Culture p. 283).

India has no national language, as Nehru thought that English could be the unifying language. But barely 10% of India knows English fluently and Hindi is spoken only in the North. Yet, very few seem to realise that India possesses in Sanskrit the Mother of all languages, so intricate, so subtle, so rich, that no other speech can equal it today. It could easily become the unifying language of India : "Sanskrit ought still to have a future as the language of the learned and it will not be a good day for India when the ancient tongues cease entirely to be written or spoken", Sri Aurobindo admonished 50 years ago. A dead language, you say! Impossible to revive? But that's what they argued about Hebrew. And did not the Jewish people, when they got back their land in 1948, revive their 'dead' language, so that it is spoken today by all Jewish people and has become alive again ? The same thing ought to be done with Sanskrit, but as Sri Aurobindo points out: "it must get rid of the curse of the heavy pedantic style contracted by it in its decline, with the lumbering impossible compounds and the overweight of hair-splitting erudition". Let the scholars begin now to revive and modernise the Sanskrit language; it would be a sure sign of the dawning of the Renaissance of India. In a few years it should be taught as the second language in schools throughout the country, with the regional language as the first and English as the third. On top of that, Sanskrit would be a gift to the world, because it will boost the studies of the Vedas, whose great secrets will be unravelled. And again, this will go in enhancing India's self image and help her to evolve a " true India".

Education of course has to be totally revamped. The kind of Westernised education which is standard in India does have its place, because India wants to be on par with the rest of the world, and Indian youth should be able to deal confidently with the West: do business, talk, and relate to a universal world culture. But nevertheless, the first thing that Indian children should be taught is the greatness of their own culture. They should learn to revere the Vedas, they should be taught the greatness of the Mahabharata and the Ramanayana; they should be told that in this country everything has been done, that it was an unsurpassed civilisation, when the West was still mumbling its first words, that Indian civilisation reached dizzying heights, which have been since unsurpassed. But overall they should be taught early that India's greatness is her spirituality, her world-wide wisdom. INDIA'S NEW EDUCATION HAS TO BE SPIRITUALISED. IT HAS TO BE AN INNER EDUCATION WHICH TEACHES TO LOOK AT THINGS FROM THE INNER PRISM, NOT THROUGH THE WESTERN ARTIFICIAL LOOKING GLASS. India's Dharma, her eternal quest for truth, should be drilled in the child from an early age. And from this firm base, everything then can be taught, from the most modern forms of mathematics, to the latest technologies.

"National education...may be described as the education which, starting with the past and making full use of the present, builds up a great nation. Whoever wishes to cut off the nation from its past, is no friend of our national growth. Whoever fails to take advantage of the present, is losing us the battle of life. We must therefore save for India all that she has stored up of knowledge, character and noble thoughts in her immemorial past. We must acquire for her the best knowledge that Europe can give her and assimilate it to her own peculiar type of national temperament. We must introduce the best methods of teaching humanity has developed, whether modern or ancient. And all these we must harmonise into a system which will be impregnated with the spirit of self-reliance, so as to build up men and not machines". (India's Reb 36).

It should also be made clear that Indian history will have to be rewritten. If not only the Jews, but also the whole world is constantly drilled in the history of the holocaust, so as to remember and not repeat the same mistakes, definitely Indian children should be taught about the rape of their country by successive Muslim invaders and the incredible harm done to India. They should know the truth about Aurangzeb, Babar and Mahmud of Ghazni, instead of the present semi-glorifying of the great Mughal culture and period. They should not be taught to hate their fellow Muslims in India, but only to know them in their real historical perspective. A certain effort in that direction has already been made by the present Government which has replaced some of the staunch Marxists, such as Romila Thapar, from the Indian Council of Research. But inspite of the outcry in the "secular" press it has triggered, a lot more needs to be done.

For instance, the Independence story should be rewritten and true nationalists given their right place. The Congress should be granted its just share of the movement, but not sanctified as it is now. All Marxist denigration of India should also be banned from the books. Indian students should be taught to look at the world through the Indian prism and see historical events, such as the rape of the Third World by Spanish conquistadors, or the colonising and impoverishment of Africa, in their factual colours.

Another symbol of the emergence of a new India will be the universal acceptance of Vande Mataram as the national anthem – we have seen in 1999 the farcical reaction of education ministers from different states when the Saraswati Vandanam was played at a function presided over by Murli Manohar Joshi. But why should anyone object to Saraswati, the Goddess of learning, She who bestowed so much Grace on India. In 1939, a disciple had said to Sri Aurobindo that: "there are some people who object to the singing of Vande Mataram as a national song; Sri Aurobindo had replied: "in that case Hindus should give up their culture". But the disciple had continued: "the argument is that the song speaks of Hindu gods, like Durga and that it is offensive to Muslims". Said Sri Aurobindo: "but it is not a religious song, it is a national song and the Durga spoken of is India as the Mother. Why should not the Muslims accept it? In the Indian concept of nationality, the Hindu view should be naturally there. If it cannot find a place, the Hindus may as well be asked to give-up their culture. The Hindus don't object to "Allah-Ho-Akbar".

Without

Let us again hear Sri Aurobindo's message on the 15th of August 1947 : " India is free, but she has not achieved unity, only a fissured and broken freedom...The whole communal division into Hindu and Muslim seems to have hardened into the figure of a permanent political division of the country. It is to be hoped that the Congress and the Nation will not accept the settled fact as for ever settled, or as anything more than a temporary expedient. For if it lasts, India may be seriously weakened, even crippled; civil strife may remain always possible, possible even a new invasion and foreign conquest. The partition of the country must go...For without it the destiny of India might be seriously impaired and frustrated. That must not be."

This was indeed prophetic and we have to understand that as long as this partition remains, we will have Kashmir, Ayodhya and the spectre of a nuclear war between the two erstwhile brothers. In SAARC, South Asia possesses the basic framework for an eventual reunification in a lose confederation, where each will keep its own identity and freedom while uniting in key economic, political and military issues like the United Europe is starting to do now. The question is: how? It certainly cannot be done in a day and it cannot be accomplished in a hurried and artificial manner. First there has to be an understanding among the people, an acceptance of that possibility, which up to now has not even been thought of seriously. Once the idea has started to be accepted by people, the process may begin - at the heart of the matter, where things are most difficult between India and Pakistan: in Kashmir, for instance.

For Kashmir represents the perfect impossibility, the absolute dead-end, and symbolises the irrevocable enmity between Pakistan and India. India will not surrender Kashmir, because she considers rightly that it has been part of her territory for 5000 years. Pakistan will not surrender its claim on the Valley, because it estimates rightly that the Kashmir vale is 95% Muslim and that under the (mad) logic of partition, it should have reverted to Islamabad. And both countries are trying by force, the one openly, the other covertly, to stake their claims on Kashmir. Thus, there is no issue except war, a nuclear conflict maybe - and everyone will be the loser: who will have Kashmir then if there is nothing left of India and Pakistan?

If the absurdity of the whole Kashmir business is seen

in that light, then India and Pakistan might agree to sit down and hammer out, not an idiotic splitting in two of Kashmir, as they have already done to India, which will solve nothing and only postpone a later confrontation, but a just reunion. LET BOTH INDIA AND PAKISTAN ADMINISTER KASHMIR, which would retain its identity and culture as a member of a greater Indian confederation. It can start in a gradual way with military observers of both the countries being posted to watch over the peace process. Eventually it can lead to a joint government of Kashmir. Then there could be a tentative reunification of both the Kashmirs, which would be a prelude to an eventual reunification of India and Pakistan, in a loose confederation of which the Kashmir joint experiment would be the model and the guinea pig, because we have no illusion that this will be an easy process.

Chapter 16

India - The Spiritual Leader of the World

"Arise O India and be proud once more of Thyself", one would be tempted to say in conclusion. This should be India's motto for the Third Millennium, after five centuries of self-denial. For, in spite of its poverty, in spite of the false Aryan invasion, in spite of the Muslim holocaust, in spite of European colonialism, in spite of Macaulay's children, in spite of the Partition, in spite of the Chinese threat, in spite of the westernised framework, India still has tremendous potential. Everything is there, ready to be manifested again, ready to mould India in to a new modern nation, a super power of the 21st century. Of course, India has to succeed in its industrialisation, it has to liberalise, because unless you can compete economically with the West, no nation can become a super power. India has also to solve its political problems, settle its separatist troubles, get rid of corruption and bureaucracy. And lastly, it has to quickly apply its mind and genius to its ecological problems, because the environment in India is in a very bad way, near the point of no-return. Thus, if India becomes a force to be reckoned with militarily, economically and socially, then the wonder that IS India could again manifest itself.

And what is this Wonder ? Beyond the image of poverty, of backwardness, beyond even the wonder that is Hinduism, there is a Knowledge – spiritual, occult, esoteric, medical even – still alive today in India. This Knowledge was once roaming upon the shores of this world - in Egypt, Mesopotamia,

Greece – but it has now vanished to be replaced by religions, with their dogmas and rituals, do's and dont's, hells and heavens. For we have lost the truth; we have lost the Great Sense, the meaning of our evolution, the meaning of why so much suffering, why dying, why getting born, why this earth, who are we, what is the soul, what is reincarnation, what is the ultimate reality of the world and the universe... But India has kept this truth, India has managed to preserve it through seven millenniums of pitfalls, of genocides and attempts at killing her Santanam Dharma.

And this will be India's gift to this planet during this century: to restore to the world its true sense, to recharge humanity with the real meaning and spirit of life, to gift to this dolorous planet That which is beyond mind: the Supra-Mental. India will become the spiritual leader of the world: "It is this religion that I am raising-up before the world, it is this that I have perfected and developed through the rishis, saints, and avatars, and now it is going forth to do my work among the nations. I am raising forth this nation to send forth my word...When therefore it is said that India shall rise, it is the Santana Dharma that shall rise, it is the Santana Dharma that shall be great. When it is said that India shall expand and extend herself, it is the Santana Dharma that shall expand and extend itself over the world. It is for the Dharma and by the Dharma that India exists". (India's Reb. p. 46 - Uttara speech).

This knowledge does not necessarily reside in mystical realms, but in authentic Indian traditional forms of genius which can be very practical. Take for example ancient medical systems, like Ayurveda, or Siddha. Today, alleopathic medicines are found even in India's remotest villages, making people dependant on harmful drugs which are expensive and only serve to enrich the big foreign multinationals. It takes a Deepak Chopra, an Indian doctor exiled in the United States, to remind the world that Ayurveda is one of the greatest medical systems ever devised; that 5000 years ago, when the rest of the planet lived in total medical ignorance, Indian doctors were already performing plastic surgery, knew that the origin of many diseases was psychosomatic, had found in mother nature the cure for most of man's ailments and realised that the five natural elements have to be balanced in the human body for a perfect harmonious life. Not only that, but Indian doctors were also yogis. They perceived that beyond the human body was another divine reality, of which the soul was the vehicle on earth. Today, Western doctors (and many Indian ones) are totally ignorant of the different planes of consciousness which superimpose our terrestrial life. Hence these doctors and the psychiatrists of the West are, as Sri Aurobindo pointed out, "searching with a torch light in the dark caverns of man's Unconscious". This ancient knowledge is unfortunately now being neglected. As a result, American companies are patenting medicines using the properties of neem or haldi, for instance, which were known 4000 years ago by India's forefathers. As in the case of Sanskrit, the Indian Government should thus put its energies and resources towards the reviving of Ayurveda.

Or take pranayama, the science of breathing. The effects of pranayama have been studied for thousands of years and Indian teachers know exactly what results this type of exercise will have on you and what kind of routine you should have to improve a particular problem or develop a certain faculty in you. Pranayama, in Sanskrit, means breath and in India it is known that prana circulates in the whole body and that one breathes not only through the nose and mouth, but through ANY part of the body, thus making prana flow everywhere. According to yogis, prana can revitalise all those parts of our body which do not receive enough energy and which, as a consequence, become weak and lose their vitality, like the eyes for instance. Pranayama is in fact everywhere: in the air which surrounds us, but also in animals, in nature, in the mineral world even. It is also found in food : today, one speaks of vitamins, proteins, calories - but one does not understand that it is actually the prana in the food which gives us energy; and the quality of this prana depends on the sort of food we eat.

Recently, this ancient knowledge was scientifically verified when the National Institute of Neuroscience in Bangalore, one of the most reputed in Asia, studied, for the fist time in the world, the effects of pranayama on 80 patients suffering from various psychological problems: depression, anorexia, insomnia, obesity, alcoholism. To do so, half of the patients continued to receive normal treatment: electric shocks, sedation, psychiatric help, while the other half was made to practise only pranayama two hours a day for three months. By using the P300 method (Positive Electrical Wave) to measure the reactions of the brain, through electrodes placed on different parts of the body, the doctors were able to study, in nano-volts, thirty milliseconds after the stimulation, the auditory and somatic reactions of the patients. They quickly noticed that the latent periods - that is the delay between the stimulus and the response of the subject - decrease considerably after the pranayama exercises and they also noted a slowing down of the breathing and the cardiac rhythm. After three months, the forty patients who only practised pranayama showed so much improvement that they were allowed to go home, while the forty others stayed on in the hospital.

Pranayama is probably the best suited Indian yogic discipline for the West, because it is so down to earth, so scientific: there are no miracles, no levitation, no smoky mysticism, as everything can be explained in a rational way. And again, the U.S.A., always prompt to experience new techniques, is using this knowledge: quite a few American companies have included exercises of pranayama in the "peps" sessions of their executives; sportsmen too are experimenting with it to improve their performances, as the film "the Great

Blue" has shown, when the hero does a series of breathing exercises known in India as "Viloma", to store as much air as possible in his lungs, before breaking a world record in underwater diving without oxygen. Today, thanks to Sri Sri Ravi Shankar, the ancient science of pranayama is not only being revived, but it is travelling all over the world, care of the Art of Living Foundation. Who then, is Sri Sri Ravi Shankar?

Sri Sri Ravi Shankar was born on May 13, 1956, in a religious family in Papanasam, Tamil Nadu. At the age of four he could recite the entire Bhagavad Gita and by the time he was nine years old, he had mastered the Rig-Veda. He, however, completed his traditional studies, including an advanced degree in modern science, before being noticed in 1975 by Maharishi Mahesh Yogi, the guru responsible for introducing meditation to the West. Maharishi took the promising youngster with him to Delhi, Rishikesh, as well as abroad, and Ravi Shankar quickly became one of his star teachers, as well as his right hand man. In 1982, after having decided to strike out on his own, Sri Sri Ravi Shankar went into ten days of silence. It is during this silence that the Sudarshan Kriya, a unique cleansing and rejuvenating process based on the repetition of different breathing rhythms, was revealed to him – and it is probably also at the same time that he received full enlightenment. And so the Art of Living was born. Today the AOL Basic course, a combination of pranayama, course points, meditation and group techniques, is taught in 132 countries and Sri Sri Ravi Shankar is a world renowned spiritual master, as well as a founding member, along with several world leaders, of the International Association for Human Values (IAHV), a Geneva-based organization that aims to re-awaken human values. He has been a featured speaker at many forums across the globe including the European Parliament, the United Nations Millennium Summit and the World Economic forum in Davos, Switzerland.

And what about Kalaripayat, a very ancient multi-faceted martial art, which is still practised in the villages of Kerala? In 522 A.D., an Indian Buddhist monk named Boddidharma, who had become a master of Kalaripayat (Buddhist monks, who travelled a lot in Asia to propagate their religion, fought bare-handed and with the bamboo stick they used for walking to defend themselves against attacks) and who was the son of the King of Kancheepuram in the state of Tamil Nadu, arrived at the court of the Chinese Emperor Liang Nuti of the 6th dynasty. The Emperor granted him an audience and gave him travel documents to walk to the Kingdom of Wei (now Junan province) at the foot of the Han Shan mountains, to a Buddhist monastery called the temple of Shaolin.

Father and founder of Zen Buddhism (called C'han in China and Dhyana in India), Boddidharma taught the Chinese monks the barehanded fighting techniques of Kalaripayat, a very ancient Indian martial art, so that they could defend themselves against the frequent attacks of bandits. In time, the monks became known all over China as skilled exponents of barehanded fighting, which came down to us as the Shaolin boxing art.

The Shaolin temple, which was handed back a few years ago to the C'han Buddhist monks by the Chinese Government, inheritors of Boddhidharma's spiritual and martial teachings, is now open to visitors. On one of its walls, one can see a fresco depicting dark-skinned Indians teaching their lighter-skinned brothers the art of barehanded fighting. On the painting is inscribed : "Tenjiku Naranokaku", which means : "the fighting techniques to train the body (which come) from India."

Kalaripayat, or Shaolin boxing, passed from China to Japan, through the Ryukyu Islands, landing in Okinawa to blossom in the art of the Empty Hand, or later, Karate. It manifested in the Japanese mainland as jiu-jiu-tso, judo,

Shorinji Kempo, etc. Karate, the art of the Empty Hand, father of all Japanese martial arts, is a blend of Boddhidharma's martial teachings and local fighting techniques, which existed there before the advent of Zen Buddhism. All Asian martial arts, particularly those of China and Japan, recognize their origin in the Shaolin Temple and honour Boddhidarma, (whom the Japanese call Dharuma). His portrait is often displayed in their dojos, where martial arts are practised.

And what about meditation, queen of all the yogic sciences? That which is above everything, without which any yogic discipline is impossible, which interiorises us, carries us within ourselves, to the discovery of our true soul and nature. There are hundreds of different mediation techniques, simple, cartesian, easy to experience, which have been devised by Indian sages since the dawn of Bharat. Each one has its own characteristics, each one gives particular results, which have been experienced by the billions of aspirants who have practised them since the dawn of Vedic times. Meditation is being practised more and more in the West and there have been numerous scientific studies, which have shown the positive effect of meditation on heart problems, psychological stress or blood circulation.

The irony is that not only do most of the Indian upper class and intellectual elite not practise meditation and pranayama, ignore Kalaripayat and not get treated with Ayurveda, but that none of these wonders are included in the schools' and universities' curriculums. So you have this wonderful knowledge, which has disappeared from the rest of the world, but if you go to cities like Delhi, or Bombay, you realise that many of the youth there have no idea about meditation, or have never heard of pranayama. They are totally cut off from their ancient culture, from the greatness of their tradition, and even look down on it. So unless Indians start taking pride in their own culture, India will never be able to gift it to the world.

Famous French writer Andre Malraux had said that unless the 21st century is spiritual, then it will not be. What he meant was that the world has now come to such a stage of unhappiness, of material dryness, of conflicts within itself, that it seems doomed and there appears no way that it can redeem itself: it is just moving towards self-destruction, - ecologically, socially, spiritually. So unless the 21st century allows a new spiritual order to take over – not a religious order, because religion has been a failure all over the world - then the world is going towards pralaya. And India holds the key to the world's future, for India is the only nation which still preserves in the darkness of Her Himalayan caves, on the luminous ghats of Benares, in the hearts of her countless yogis, or even in the minds of her ordinary folk, the key to the planetary evolution, its future and its hope.

The 21st century, will be the era of the East; this is where the sun is going to rise again, after centuries of decadence and submission to Western colonialism; this is where the focus of the world is going to shift. As in the past when India used to shine and send forth Her Dharma all over the Orient - to Japan, Thailand, China, Burma, or Cambodia - and influenced their civilizations and religions for centuries to come, she will once again emit Her light and radiate, Queen among nations: "India of the ages is not dead nor has She spoken Her last creative word; She lives and has still something to do for Herself and the human peoples. And that which She must seek now to awake, is not an anglicised oriental people, docile pupil of the West and doomed to repeat the cycle of the Occident's success and failure, but still the ancient immemorial Shakti recovering Her deepest self, lifting Her head higher towards the supreme source of light and strength and turning to discover the complete meaning and vaster form of Her Dharma".

Bibliography

* Negationism in India, by Konrad Elst, Voice of India, New Delhi.
* The Wonder That was India, by A.L. Basham, Rupa.
* Vande Mataram, by Sri Aurobindo, Sri Aurobindo Ashram Press, Pondichery.
* Histoire de l'Inde, by Jean Danielou, Editions Fayard, Paris.
* India's Rebirth, Institut de Recherches Evolutives, Paris. Distributed in India by Mira Aditi Center, 62 Sriranga 1st Cross, 4th Stage Kuvempunagar, Mysore 570023
* The Mother, by Sri Aurobindo, Sri Aurobindo Ashram Press, Pondichery.
* Life without death, by Satprem, Mira Aditi center, 62 Sriranga 1st Cross, 4th Stage Kuvempunagar, Mysore 570023
* Indigenous Indians, by Konrad Elst, Voice of India, New Delhi.
* The Foundations of Indian Culture, by Sri Aurobindo, Sri Aurobindo Ashram Press, Pondichery.
* Hindu Society under siege, by Sitaram Goel, Voice of India; New Delhi.
* The Hour of God, by Sri Aurobindo, Sri Aurobindo Ashram Press, Pondichery.
* The Supramental Manifestation, by Sri Aurobindo, Sri Aurobindo Ashram Press, Pondichery.

* The Secret of the Veda, by Sri Aurobindo, Sri Aurobindo Ashram Press, Pondichery.

* The Mother's Agenda, as recorded by Satprem, 13 volumes, Mira Aditi centre, 62 Sriranga 1st Cross, 4th Stage Kuvempunagar, Mysore 570023

* Mother India and Her destiny, by the Mother, Sri Aurobindo Ashram Press, Pondichery.

* Arise Arjuna, by David Frawley, Voice of India, 1994.

The author is grateful to the Sri Aurobindo Ashram Trust for permission to quote extensively from Sri Aurobindo and the Mother's works.

About India Research Press

India Research Press is a collectively run book publisher with support of Authors and Editors. Since our founding in 1999, we have tried to meet the needs of readers who are exploring, or are committed to the politics of change.

Our goal is to publish books that encourage critical thinking and constructive action on the key political, cultural, social, economic and ecological issues shaping life in the Indian Sub-continent and in the world.

In this way, we hope to give expression to a wide diversity of democratic and social movements.

India Research Press publishes original works as well as works under Rights with various university and academic publishers throughout the world.

The Group now has forty-five titles to its credit and many new titles scheduled for the next few months.

Since our conception, we have added two new imprints to our existing line of Academic publishing.

The group is proud to introduce its three divisions of publishing....

India Research Press

Academic publishing division.

Swankit

General division – Health, Non Fiction and Educational titles.

Tara Press

General division – Mass Market including Fiction.

The group is headed by Anuj Bahri Malhotra, its CEO & Commissioning Manager. He is assisted by an efficient and professional staff of Editors, Administrators and Office Assistants. Born into a bookseller family, running the most sought after bookshop in the country, Anuj has long inherited experience in the Indian Book Industry.

Our List of Titles

- Divided Kashmir : Old Problems, New Opportunities for India, Pakistan and the Kashmiri People.
  By: Mushtaqur Rahman
- British Conquest and Dominion of India : Two volume set.
  By: Sir Penderal Moon
- India and the Bomb : Public Opinion and Nuclear Options.
  By: David Courtright & Amitabh Mattoo
- Rural Labour Relations in India.
  By: T.J.Byres & Karin Kapadia
- Architecture of Indian Desert: [Illus in Colour & B/W]
  By: Kulbhushan & Minakshi Jain
- Central Asia : A travelers companion.
  By: Katherine Hopkirk [distribution only]
- Rogue States : The Rule of Force in World Affairs.
  By: Noam Chomsky
- Stolen Harvest : The Hijacking of the Global Food Supply.
  By: Vandana Shiva
- Heaven's Child and other Poems
  By: Sameer Kak
- Natural Resource Management and Institutional Change.
  An ODI/IRP joint series.
  By: Diana Carney and John Farrington
- Development as process. An ODI/IRP joint series.
  By: David Mosse, John Farrington and Alan Rew.
- Quiz Master India. Volume 1
  By: Sanjay Sharma
- Quiz Master India. Volume 2
  By: Sanjay Sharma
- ....and the answer is a pineapple
  By: Claudia Hyles
- Lahore 1947 : The last days of Lahore at Partition
  By: Ahmed Salim., Intro by : Ian Talbot
- Democracy-a failure, Shefocracy-the solution, for human welfare.
  By: Dr. Rabin Mukherjee

- India-Sri Lanka relations and Sri Lanka's Ethnic Conflict Documents : 1947-2000. [set of 5 volumes]
  By: Dr. Avtar Singh Bhasin
- Security in the New Millenium : Views from South Asia
  By: Rajesh M. Basrur
- The Saffron Book : A study of the Saffron politics.
  By: Prafull Goradia
- Roots of Rhetoric : Politics of Nuclear Weapons in India & Pakistan
  By: Haider K. Nizamani
- Democracy and Dictatorship in South Asia : Dominant Classes and Political Outcomes in India, Pakistan and Bangladesh
  By: Robert W. Stern
- Quiz Master India : A Student's guide to Success [omnibus]
  By: Sanjay Sharma.
- Partition and Gnocide Manifestation of Violence In Punjab
  By : Anders Bjorn Hansen
- Vegetarian Indian Cooking
  By : Manju Kumari Singh
- Sniffing Papa (Fiction)
  By : Inderjeet Badhwar
- Water Wars : Privatization, Pollution, and Profit
  By : Vandana Shiva
- Beyond Turk And Hindu
  By : Gilmartin and Lawrence
- Arena of Laughter...Set of Two Volumes
  By : Sudhir Nath
- The Muslims of the Indian Sub-Continent and of the Diaspora After the Attacks of September 11
  By : Frédéric Grare
- SAARC in the Twenty-First Century: Towards a Cooperative Future
  By : Dipankar Banerjee
- South Asia and the War on Terrorism : Analysing the Implications of 11 September
  By : Dipankar Banerjee and Gert W. Kueck
- Letters Against the War
  By : Tiziano Terzani
- Thematic Space in Indian Architecture
  By : Kulbhushan Jain

Our Forthcoming Titles

- Hanklyn-Janklin : A rumble-tumble of Indian Words used in everyday English.
  By: Nigel Hankin
- Pakistan : In the Face of the Afghan Conflict 1979-1985
  By : Frédéric Grare
- The Sustainable Livelihood Series :
  An ODI/IRP joint series
  Volume One / Volume Two / Volume Three........ [continuing series]
- Katha Sagar : A collection of Prem Chand's Stories
  By: R. Gupta
- Industrial Growth in the Punjab Since Indiependence :
  A Historical Inquiry 1947 to the Present
  By: Gurpreet K. Chowdhary
- Slow & Steady Get Me Ready
  By: June R. Oberlander
- Adultery and other stories
  By: Farrukh Dhondy
- India's National Security Annual Review 2002
  By: Satish Kumar
- Cricket the essentials of the game
  By: Sir Richard Hadlee
- No Curtains Yet
  By: V.K. Madhavan Kutty

For further information, write to........

India Research Press
Publisher
B-4/22, Safdarjung Enclave, New Delhi – 110 029.
Phone : 4694610; Fax : 4618637
www.indiaresearch press.com   e-mail : bahrisons@vsnl.com

{ India Research Press   **SwanKit**   TARA press